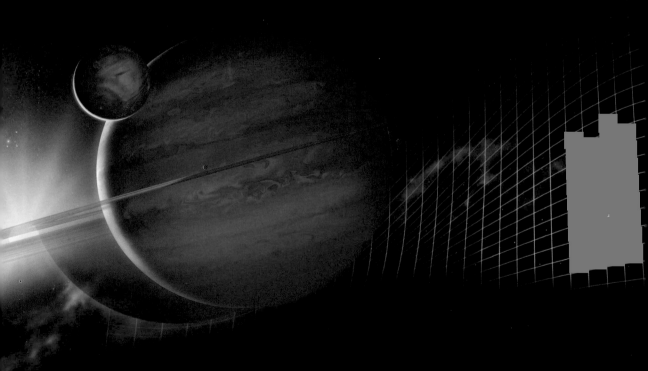

The Heavens Declare Creation
and Science Confirms It

Taking Back
Astronomy

Jason Lisle

Ph.D. in Astrophysics from the University of Colorado

Taking Back Astronomy

Ninth Printing: June 2022

For information write: Master Books P.O. Box 726, Green Forest, AR 72638
Master Books® is a division of the New Leaf Publishing Group, Inc.

Printed in China

Cover by Brent Spurlock and interior design by Bryan Miller

ISBN-13: 978-0-89051-471-9
ISBN-13: 978-1-61458-282-3 (digital)

Library of Congress Number: 2006923462

Please visit our website for other great titles:
www.masterbooks.com

For information regarding author interviews,
please contact the publicity department at (870)-438-5288

Please consider requesting that a copy of this volume be purchased by your local library system.

Master Books®
A Division of New Leaf Publishing Group
www.masterbooks.com

Table of Contents

Acknowledgments

This book would not have been possible without the support of many friends and my family. I want to extend a special thanks to the reviewers and technical consultants of this book. These are Danny Faulkner, Ken Ham, Russ Humphreys, Jonathan Sarfati, and Carl Wieland. Their encouragement and feedback are very much appreciated.

About the Author

Dr. Jason Lisle graduated summa cum laude from Ohio Wesleyan University where he double-majored in physics and astronomy and minored in mathematics. He received his master's degree and Ph.D. in astrophysics from the University of Colorado in Boulder. Dr. Lisle has done extensive research in solar astrophysics at JILA (Joint Institute for Laboratory Astrophysics) using the Solar and Heliospheric Observatory (SOHO) spacecraft. His doctoral dissertation "Probing the Dynamics of Solar Supergranulation and Its Interaction with Magnetism" explored the nature of solar subsurface weather, convection, large-scale solar flows, and near-surface magnetism.

Dr. Lisle began working in full-time apologetics ministry, focusing on the defense of Genesis. He was instrumental in developing the planetarium at the Creation Museum in Kentucky, writing and directing popular planetarium shows, including "The Created Cosmos."

His scientific discoveries include the following: the detection of polar alignment of supergranulation, the cause of the large-scale disk convergence anomaly seen in correlation tracking of solar Doppler data, the detection of solar giant cell boundaries, and the cause of the "wavelike" characteristics seen in solar power spectra. He has also made contributions in the field of general relativity, having developed a novel technique for computing trajectories in the Schwarzschild metric with subsequent application in other metrics.

As Director of Research, Dr. Lisle currently leads the gifted team of scientists at the Institute for Creation Research (ICR) who investigate and demonstrate the evidence for creation. As a creation scientist, Dr. Lisle effectively communicates a broad range of topics from in-depth presentations of distant starlight, Einstein's relativity, and problems with the big bang to topics from astronomy, general science, apologetics, and dinosaurs.

Books and DVDs by Dr. Jason Lisle include:

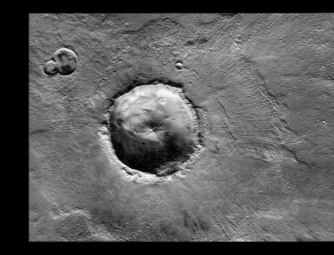

Created Cosmos (DVD)

Creation Astronomy (DVD)

Distant Starlight (DVD)

Taking Back Astronomy

Old-Earth Creationism on Trial

Ultimate Proof of Creation

Discerning Truth

Stargazers Guide to the Night Sky

I NTRODUCTION

the person did not really vanish. Notice that we do not draw this conclusion because of what we actually saw, but rather because it is the only explanation that is compatible with our world view. Our beliefs have affected our interpretation of the evidence.

A very young child might draw an entirely different conclusion. Perhaps she does not yet have enough experience to know that people do not possess the power to make something vanish. Or perhaps she understands

INTRODUCTION

Each of us has a world view — a way of thinking about the world in which we live. We all have certain beliefs: ideas that we hold to be true. These beliefs affect how we see the world and how we interpret the things we experience.

For example, most of us believe that things cannot simply cease to exist. So when we see a magician make someone disappear, we know that it is merely a trick. Perhaps a trap door exists which we can't see. Perhaps it is a trick using light and mirrors. In any case,

that most people cannot do this, but she thinks that maybe magicians can. In any case, because she has a different world view than we do, she draws a different conclusion: the magician can make people vanish! Our world view prevents us from drawing that conclusion — even though we have witnessed exactly the same event. We both have the same evidence, but we have a different interpretation.

A world view is really a kind of bias. It prevents us from being objective and "open-minded" about certain things.

That's not always a bad thing. In the

above example, our world view helped us to draw the correct conclusion because we were unwilling to consider the absurd possibility that the person really vanished. The less-experienced child draws an incorrect conclusion, because she has an incorrect bias. A correct world view/bias can help us draw correct conclusions about the evidence. An incorrect world view/bias can prevent us from drawing correct conclusions.

In a way, a world view is like having "mental glasses." Many people wear corrective lenses to help them see the world better. Without these glasses, the world appears blurry, but with the glasses in place, the world snaps into focus and things become clear.

Each of us wears "mental glasses" — we all have a world view. That's because we don't know everything; we are not aware of all of the evidence, all of the facts. We require a world view to fill in the missing pieces, and to make sense of what we experience.

However, it is crucially important that we have the right world view. Glasses of the wrong prescription can make the world appear even blurrier than it otherwise would. Glasses can either distort or make clear, and so can a world view. So which world view gives us the best perception of reality? On what foundation should we base our thinking, so that we can draw correct conclusions from the evidence we observe?

The Bible claims to be the authoritative Word of God. If an all-powerful, all-knowing God did indeed give us the Bible by inspiring men to write it, then Scripture would certainly provide a solid foundation for our way of thinking. The Bible provides answers to the most important questions people ask: What is the purpose of our existence? How did this world come about? What happens when we die? Why is there death and suffering in the world? How should we live?

Furthermore, the Bible is a history book which has demonstrated its accuracy time and time again. When it comes to matters of origins, it makes sense to consult an accurate history book, one recorded by eyewitnesses. Ultimately, we can base our beliefs about origins on the Word of God, or the speculations of other human beings. When it comes to the details of the creation of the universe, we can choose to trust God (who was there), or man (who was not).

This is the heart of the creation versus evolution debate. Many people think the debate is about evidence, and although the evidence is important, evidence is always interpreted through a person's world view. So the debate is really about world views. The debate is over which interpretation of the evidence is best. Think about it this way: both creationists and evolutionists have the same evidence. They have access to the same fossils and the same rocks. They study the same principles of genetics, chemistry, and physics. They observe the same universe. Why then do they draw such different conclusions when it comes to matters of origins? Ultimately, it is because they have different world views, and so they interpret the same evidence differently.

The heart of the issue is whether we start from the foundation of the Bible, or

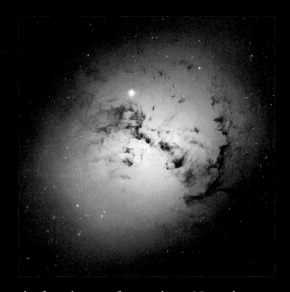

the foundation of naturalism. Naturalism is the belief that there is nothing outside of "nature" — the world we see, with its matter and energy, is all that exists, so it must have created itself by its own processes and properties. There is no supernatural realm in this world view. Many scientists today, even though they themselves might believe in God, seem to regard this as irrelevant to the way they think about the origin and history of the world.

For all practical purposes, therefore, they are operating within a naturalistic framework, a belief system that rejects God.

Many critics have suggested that we should not start from the Bible — that this is unscientific. However, if the Bible really is absolutely true, if it really is accurate history, wouldn't it be unscientific to ignore this information? Is it logical to deny recorded history, and choose to rely instead on guesswork? Since all scientific evidence must be interpreted in light of some world view, it seems very reasonable to base our world view on the infallible Word of the Creator. I have found that the Bible is a sure foundation for a world view that is logical, moral, self-consistent, and consistent with the evidence.

Many books have been written which show that the scientific evidence is consistent with what the Bible teaches. These resources have shown that biology, geology, paleontology, and anthropology make sense when interpreted through the lenses of Scripture. Many of these resources are available through our website at *answersingenesis.org*. However, currently, very few resources exist which interpret evidences in the field of astronomy from a biblical creation perspective.

The purpose of this book is to provide a starting point in the field of creation astronomy. When we understand the evidence, we will see that it makes sense in light of Scripture. The observations in astronomy are con-

sistent with what the Bible teaches. We will begin by exploring how the astonishing size and beauty of the universe testify to God's glory. We will then explore passages of the Bible which touch on astronomy. These passages are consistent with what is known about the universe.

We will also deal with passages of Scripture which conflict with the current opinion of the majority of scientists. One important area of conflict is the age of the universe; most astronomers believe that the universe is around 14 billion years old, yet the Bible indicates a much more recent origin. We will explore the reasons for the common belief in vast ages. Additionally, we will address the so-called "distant starlight problem." This is the idea that light from the most distant galaxies must take many billions of years to arrive on earth, allegedly proving that the universe is indeed billions of years old. This argument is used by critics in an attempt to disprove the Bible (or at least the biblical time scale) in favor of the big bang. However, when investigated carefully, the argument does not work. We will see that distant starlight does not support the big bang.

The age of the universe is not the only area of conflict. The Bible indicates that the universe was supernaturally created, in sharp contrast to the naturalism of the big-bang and nebular accretion models. We will also explore the idea of extra-terrestrial life. The prevailing evolutionary world view accepts alien life as more or less a given, but what does the Bible teach? When the evidence is interpreted properly, we will find that it fits with God's Word.

In the final chapter, the starting assumptions of various world views will be discussed. We will explore the internal inconsistencies of non-biblical world views, and show how

the Bible leads to a logically consistent world view in which science and technology are possible. We will also discuss the non-material implications of starting from Scripture — the divinely inspired Word of God.

This book also contains in-depth sections which contain material of a more detailed nature. Readers with an interest in the scientific details may find these sections helpful. By design, the in-depth sections are not essential to the main points of the book; so, feel free to skim or skip these sections as desired.

In this book, we will see that the Bible is accurate when it touches on astronomy. The Bible provides a logical foundation for the interpretation of scientific evidence in the field of astrophysics, as it does for other fields of science. We will see that the evidence makes sense when we view the universe through biblical glasses. We are "taking back" the field of astronomy; we are giving the universe back to the Lord who created it.

hese images were captured from 1996 to 2000, and show Saturn's rings open up from just past edge-on to nearly fully open as it moves from autumn towards winter in its Northern Hemisphere.

Helix nebula

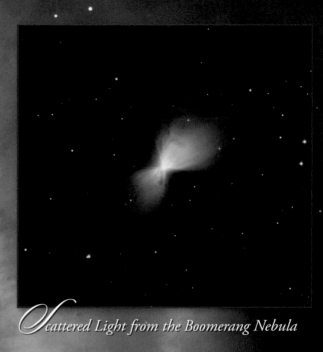

Scattered Light from the Boomerang Nebula

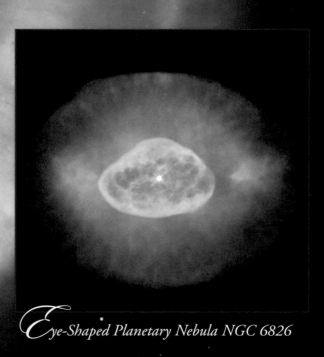

Eye-Shaped Planetary Nebula NGC 6826

CHAPTER ONE

The splendor of God's creation

Hubble deep field

Crab nebula

The heavens declare the glory of God; the skies proclaim the work of his hands" (NIV). This beautiful statement from Psalm 19:1 indicates one of the purposes of the created universe: the universe reveals the majesty of its Creator. Of course, God's glory can be seen in many different aspects of creation — not just the heavens. Consider the magnificent intricacy of a living cell, the complexity and the amazing diversity of life on earth, and the mathematical precision of the laws of physics and chemistry. These are all indicative of the incomprehensible creativity, intelligence, and power of the Creator.

Why then does the Bible single out the heavens as declaring His glory? Perhaps the heavens declare God's glory in a special way or to a greater extent. It may even be that the starry universe was specially designed for the purpose of declaring God's glory to us. We will see that the universe has incredible beauty. This alone would be sufficient reason to praise God for His creation, but not only did God make the universe beautiful, He made it unimaginably large. The range of scales in the universe is truly staggering. The universe contains objects of incredible size and mass at distances which the human mind cannot fully grasp. When we consider the power of the Lord who made all this, we cannot help but feel humbled. Truly, the God who created this universe is glorious and worthy of praise. Let us now explore the size and beauty of the universe to gain an appreciation for the majesty of the Creator.

Let's start close to home, with a relatively small astronomical object. The moon is the nearest (natural) celestial body. It is approximately 2,100 miles (3,400 kilometers) in diameter — roughly the size of the

The moon is about the same size as the United States of America.

continental United States (see below). The moon orbits at an average distance of 240,000 miles (380,000 km) from the earth. On the one hand, this is a tremendous distance. On the other hand, it is not so far as to be totally incomprehensible; some cars have as many miles on them as this. The moon orbits the earth in a roughly circular path, taking about one month from start to finish. In fact, that is where we get the idea for a "month." According to Scripture, one of the reasons God created the celestial bodies was to be for signs, seasons, days, and years (Gen. 1:14) — in other words, to mark the passage of time. The moon does just that. It continually orbits the earth every month with clockwork precision.

Additionally, the moon (the "lesser light" created on day 4) was designed to "rule the night," according to Genesis 1:16. Indeed, the moon does rule the night; it outshines every other nighttime celestial object. In fact, when the moon is out, it has a tendency to "wash out" most other astronomical objects, making them more difficult to see. This effect is particularly evident when the moon is near its full phase. At that time, the moon is over 2,500 times brighter than the next brightest nighttime object (Venus).

Let us move farther out into space, and consider the "greater light" that God created on day 4 — the sun. The sun (like other stars) is a glowing hot ball of hydrogen gas. It derives energy from the fusion of hydrogen to helium in the core. The sun is effectively a

The sun is about 400 times more distant than the moon. Remarkably, it is also 400 times larger. So it has the same angular size as the moon[1] — meaning it appears the same size and covers the same portion of the sky. It is interesting that God made both of the "great lights" the same angular size — and far larger (in angle) than any of the other celestial objects. There is no naturalistic reason why the sun and moon would be at

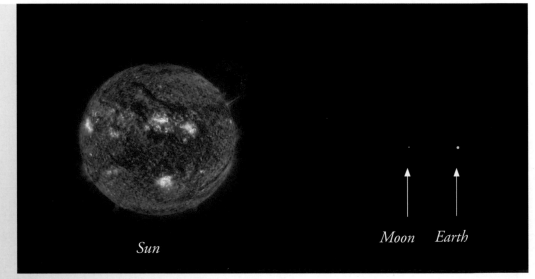

The relative size of the sun, moon, and Earth.

stable hydrogen bomb. It is an extremely efficient source of energy, placed at just the right distance to provide the right amount of light and heat for the earth.

just the right distances to have the same apparent size as seen from earth. As far as we know, the earth is the only planet for which this is the case.[2]

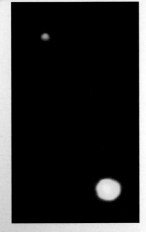

Pluto and its moon Charon

The sun is over 100 times the diameter of the earth (page 16). If it were hollow, it could hold over 1 million earths. At first, it seems almost "wasteful" to create such a massive globe merely to provide light for earth: until we consider that God created the sun just as easily as the rest of the universe. It wasn't at all difficult for Him (Jer. 32:17) and it demonstrates His great power. At the incredible distance of 93 million miles (150 million km), we cannot fully appreciate just how far away the sun is. An analogy may be helpful. How long would it take to drive 93 million miles? If we were to drive 65 miles per hour (105 km/hr), it would take 163 years to drive this distance. We couldn't drive this far in our lifetime.

The sun is far from the earth, and yet the earth is much closer to the sun than many of the other planets. Consider Pluto, a tiny frozen world at the outer edge of the planets of the solar system. Pluto (on average) is about 40 times farther away from the sun than the earth is. Traveling at 65 miles per hour, it would take about 6,500 years to reach Pluto. This is comparable to the age of the universe. The solar system is truly vast; if it had been the only thing God had made, we should certainly be impressed. Yet, God has created on even larger scales. Consider the distances between the stars.

Let's start with the nearest star system to the earth (besides the sun), the Alpha Centauri system (see page 19, bottom). Unlike the solar system, Alpha Centauri contains more than one star. Two bright stars (comparable to the sun in size and color) revolve

Globular Star Cluster M80

(3.8 mm) away from the sun. The sun itself would be smaller than the period at the end of this sentence. Where would we place the next nearest star in our one-foot scale model solar system? At this scale, Alpha Centauri would be over half a mile (about one km) away, and that's just the nearest star system. Our galaxy is comprised of countless numbers of stars at much greater distances. Using our one-foot scale model solar system, the galaxy would be larger than the Pacific Ocean!

Our galaxy is shaped like a disk with a bulge in the center. Earth is located in the disk, closer to the edge than the center. The disk has spiral arms; we cannot directly see this

around each other every 80 years. A third faint red dwarf star called "Proxima" lies farther away. The distance to this system is about 25 trillion miles. Such a number has little meaning to most of us; who can comprehend 25 trillion miles? This is about 6,800 times farther away from the earth than Pluto is.

To help grasp this to some extent, let's imagine that we had a miniature scale model of the solar system with Pluto's orbit being only one foot (about 30 cm) in diameter. The sun would be approximately in the center, and the earth would be just over an eighth of an inch

Some galaxies are elliptical in shape

spiral structure because we are within it. To us, the galaxy looks like a faint cloud band stretching across the sky on (northern hemisphere) summer nights (or winter nights for the southern hemisphere). This is how our galaxy gets its name — the "Milky Way." Viewed from a distance, which of course no human being has ever done, our galaxy might look a bit like M31 — the "Andromeda Galaxy" shown at right.

Our galaxy contains over 100 billion stars; the Bible says that God calls them all by their names (Ps. 147:4, Isa. 40:26). How amazing that God has a name for each and every one of those stars! Some of these stars

Galaxy M31 (Andromeda galaxy)

are far separated from their nearest neighbor, much like the sun. Some stars come in binary or multiple star systems, such as Alpha Centauri. Some stars come in large clusters. Consider the M80 star cluster shown on the opposite page. This cluster within our galaxy is estimated to contain over 100,000 stars. That means that the Milky Way has roughly a million times as many — imagine, one million stars for every single star in this cluster!

The galaxy contains more than stars. It also contains nebulae (plural of "nebula"). These "clouds" are made of hydrogen gas —

Alpha and Beta Centauri

The Rosette Nebula

The Eagle Nebula

below is several thousand times larger than our solar system. It is incredible to realize that our solar system would not even be visible on this image. God paints

the same stuff as stars, but whereas stars are compact spheres, a nebula is spread out over a much larger region of space. When a nebula is heated by nearby stars, it glows, often with vivid and beautiful colors. Consider the beauty of the nebulae shown above, but keep in mind how enormous these objects are. The Rosette Nebula is not only beautiful, it is estimated to be more massive than 10,000 suns. The section of the Eagle Nebula shown

beautiful artwork, and He does it on a canvas of unimaginable size.

When we consider the immensity of the Milky Way, with its 100 billion stars, countless nebulae, and star clusters, the overwhelming power of the Creator becomes clear. Yet, our galaxy is not the only one. God has created innumerable galaxies with a wide range of shapes and sizes. Some galaxies are spiral, like the Milky Way and M31 (page 19, top). Others are elliptical in shape (page 18, bottom), and some galaxies have shapes that can only be described as "irregular." Many galaxies come in clusters. The Milky Way belongs to a cluster of a few dozen galaxies called the "Local Group." Some clusters are much larger than this. The Virgo cluster has about 2,000 galaxies. Clusters of galaxies are organized into even larger superclusters — clusters of clusters. Superclusters show organization on the largest scales we can currently observe; they form an intricate web of strings and voids throughout the visible universe.

Just think about the quantity of energy involved when God created all this. The sun alone gives off more energy every second than one billion major cities would produce in one year. Yet, our entire galaxy is 20 billion times more luminous than the sun.[3] It is estimated that there are at least as many galaxies as there are stars in the Milky Way (100 billion). Just consider such energy and mass filling a volume of space that is immense beyond our ability to fathom.

How does the Bible describe the creation of all this? Genesis 1:16 states simply that God "also made the stars." It is astonishing that the creation of the entire universe beyond earth is described so casually by such a simple statement. The biblical description makes it sound like the creation of all the hundreds of billions of galaxies was so trivially easy for God that it barely deserves to be mentioned. How awesome is the Lord!

When we contemplate all this which God created, it brings to mind Psalm 8:3–4: "When I consider your heavens,

the work of your fingers, the moon and the stars, which you have set in place, what is man that you are mindful of him, the son of man that you care for him?" It is amazing that the God who created such a universe would be concerned with something as small as human beings. Yet, Scripture makes it clear that human beings are very important to God. Our place in the universe is very significant, as we will see in later chapters.

Who would have thought from a casual glance at the night sky that the universe would be so majestic and so enormous? Certainly the night sky is stunningly beautiful, even to the unaided eye. Who could have known that it would contain hundreds of billions of galaxies, each with millions to trillions of stars, along with countless clusters and nebulae of immense size and breathtaking beauty? It seems that the more we zoom in on the universe, the more

beautiful it becomes, and the more we realize how truly vast and amazing it is. The more we "magnify" the universe, the more amazed we are by its beauty and complexity. The same is true of the Creator of the universe. The more we magnify God, the more we realize just how amazing He is. It seems that God has constructed the universe to reflect this aspect of His character. Romans 1:20 indicates that many of the invisible attributes of God can be understood from the things which He made, so it shouldn't surprise us that the universe is so incredible. Truly the heavens declare the glory of God and the skies proclaim the work of His hands!

For since the creation of the world God's invisible qualities—his eternal power and divine nature—have been clearly seen, being understood from what has been made, so that men are without excuse (Romans 1:20).

*R*ing galaxies are comprised of a central core surrounded by a ring of bright blue stars. Since blue stars cannot last billions of years, ring galaxies are a reminder that the universe is much younger than is generally claimed.

Distant Spiral Galaxy NGC 4603, Home to Variable Stars

Sombrero Galaxy (Messier 104)

CHAPTER TWO

The universe confirms the Bible

In this chapter, we will explore some passages of Scripture which touch upon the topics of astronomy and astrophysics. It is interesting that many of the Bible's statements about astronomy went against the generally accepted teachings of the time. Undoubtedly, many of these verses would have seemed counterintuitive, and may have been difficult to believe when they were first written. However, modern science has confirmed what the Bible has taught. As in all things, the Bible is absolutely correct when it teaches about the universe.

THE EARTH IS ROUND

The Bible indicates that the earth is round. Consider Isaiah 40:22 which mentions the "circle of the earth." This description is certainly fitting — particularly when the earth is viewed from space; the earth always appears as a circle, since it is round.

Another verse that indicates the spherical nature of our planet is Job 26:10. This verse teaches that God has inscribed a circle on the surface of the waters at the boundary of light and darkness. This boundary between light and darkness (day and night) is called the "terminator" since the light stops or "terminates" there. Someone standing on the terminator would be experiencing either a sunrise or a sunset; they are going from day to night or from night to day. The terminator is always a circle, because the earth is round.

One of the great delights of observing the moon through a small telescope is to look at its terminator, especially during the first or third quarter phases when the terminator is directly down the middle of the moon. The craters are most easily seen at this boundary since the sun is at a low angle and casts very long shadows there. The moon looks particularly three-dimensional when viewed through a telescope during these phases; it is clear that the moon is a sphere — not a flat disk (see photo below).

For the earth, the terminator occurs not on a cratered rocky surface, but primarily on water (since the earth's surface is 70 percent water). Job 26:10 suggests a "God's eye" view of the earth. This biblical passage would be nonsense if the earth were flat, since there would be no true terminator; there is no line to "step over" that separates the day from night on a flat surface. Either it is day everywhere or night everywhere on a hypothetical "flat earth." However, the earth does indeed have a boundary between light and darkness which is always a circle since the earth is round.

Curiously, many astronomy textbooks credit Pythagoras (c. 570–500 B.C.) with being the first person to assert that the earth is round.[4] However, the biblical passages are older than this.

The moon in first quarter phase

Isaiah is generally acknowledged to have been written in the 700s B.C. and Job is thought to have been written around 2000 B.C. The secular astronomers before the time of Pythagoras must have thought the Bible was wrong about its teaching of a round earth, yet the Bible was exactly right. It was the secular science of the day that needed to be corrected.

THE EARTH FLOATS IN SPACE

A very interesting verse to consider is Job 26:7 which states that God "hangs the earth on nothing." This might evoke an image of God hanging the earth like a Christmas tree ornament, but hanging it on empty space. This verse expresses (in a poetic way) the fact that the earth is unsupported by any other object — something quite unnatural for the ancient writers to imagine. Indeed, the earth does float in space. We now have pictures of the

The earth hangs on nothing.

earth taken from space that show it floating in the cosmic void. The earth literally hangs on nothing, just as the Bible teaches.

THE EXPANSION OF THE UNIVERSE

The Bible indicates in several places that the universe has been "stretched out" or expanded. For example, Isaiah 40:22 teaches that God "stretches out the heavens like a curtain, and spreads them out like a tent to dwell in." This would suggest that the universe has actually increased in size since its creation. God has stretched it out. He has expanded it (and is perhaps still expanding it). This verse must have seemed very strange when it was first written. The universe certainly doesn't look as if it is expanding. After all, if you look at the night sky tonight, it will appear about the same size as it did the previous night, and the night before that. Ancient star maps appear virtually identical to the night sky today. Could the universe really have been expanded? It must have been hard to believe at the time.

In fact, secular scientists once believed that the universe was eternal and unchanging. The idea of an expanding universe would have been considered nonsense to most scientists of the past. It must have been tempting for Christians to reject what the Bible teaches about the expansion of the universe. Perhaps some Christians tried to "reinterpret" Isaiah 40:22, and read it in an unnatural way so that they wouldn't have to believe in an expanding universe. When the world believes one thing, and the Bible teaches another, it is always tempting to think that God got the details wrong, but God is never wrong.

Most astronomers today believe that the universe is expanding. This expansion is a very natural result of the physics that Einstein discovered — general relativity. Moreover, there is observational evidence that the universe is indeed expanding. In the 1920s, astronomers discovered that virtually all clusters of galaxies appear to be moving away from all other clusters (see creation in-depth box); this indicates that the entire universe is expanding.

This effect can be illustrated with points on a balloon. As the balloon is inflated, all points move farther away from each other (see illustration at left). If the entire universe were being stretched out, the galaxies would all be moving away; and that is exactly what they appear to be doing. It is interesting that the Bible recorded the notion of an expanding universe thousands of years before secular science came to accept the idea.

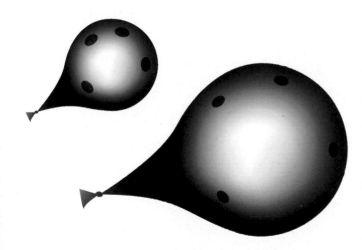

Balloon illustration

The Hubble Law: what does it mean?

Nearly all galaxies in the universe are "redshifted." That means that the wavelengths of the light they emit have been increased. The light has been stretched out since it was emitted — it is shifted toward the red end of the spectrum (since red light has a longer wavelength than blue).

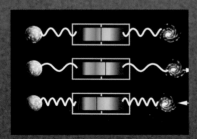

Doppler effect

There are several ways in which light can be redshifted. Motion is one way; this is called the "Doppler effect." When a car passes by, its sound changes pitch because the sound waves are either compressed or stretched out depending on whether the car is approaching or moving away.

Likewise, the wavelength of light is changed when the source is moving. The effect is not as easy to see with light as it is to hear with sound. Since the speed of light is so much greater than the speed of sound, objects must be moving very fast in order to see the Doppler effect.

Gravity can also affect the wavelength of light. Strong gravitational fields slow the passage of time in accordance with Einstein's relativity. This means that light emitted near a massive object will be redshifted. Expansion of the universe can also cause light to be redshifted. As the universe expands, any light traveling within it will also be stretched out along with the universe. The longer the light has been traveling, the more redshifted it will be.

Astronomers can determine the distances to galaxies, and are also able to determine the redshifts of those galaxies. Observations have shown that the redshift of a galaxy is proportional to its distance from our galaxy. The more distant a galaxy is, the more its light is shifted toward the red; this is called the "Hubble law." Most astronomers believe that expansion of the universe is the most likely cause for the redshifts, because it would naturally lead to this result: more distant galaxies would be more redshifted because their light has been traveling longer and has thus been expanded by a greater amount. The "Hubble law" is the evidence — distant galaxies show greater redshifts than nearby galaxies. The interpretation is that universal expansion has caused these redshifts.

Recently, some astronomers have questioned this interpretation. Might there be another cause of these redshifts? This is certainly possible. However, there are some good reasons to think that universal expansion is the correct interpretation of the Hubble law. First of all, a static universe is nearly impossible according to general relativity. The laws of physics indicate that the universe must either be expanding or collapsing, so we would expect the universe to be expanding (or possibly collapsing) on the basis of known physics — even if we had no observations of redshifts at all. Secondly, other known ways of producing redshifts would not necessarily produce a Hubble law relation. Expansion of the universe naturally produces the result that more distant galaxies are more redshifted — all on the basis of known physics. I would suggest that expansion of the universe is the best explanation of the data at the moment, though other interpretations are possible.

An expanding universe does not necessarily support the big bang. Just because the universe is apparently expanding does not mean that it was ever infinitely small; nor does this indicate that a big bang caused the expansion. It is also important to note that the big bang did not predict any such expansion. On the contrary, the big bang was invented to explain such expansion within the framework of naturalism. The Bible, however, did refer to an expanding universe — long before secular astronomers came to accept that idea.

Conservation of Mass-Energy

A very important concept in physics is the conservation of energy. This principle states that energy cannot be created nor destroyed. There are a lot of different kinds of energy; heat, light, sound, and electricity are all forms of energy. We can change one type of energy into another and we can move energy from one place to another, but the total quantity of energy in the universe is constant and cannot be changed.

There is also a conservation principle of mass. Mass is the property of an object to resist a change in its motion. Things that possess a lot of mass are very heavy; things with little mass are light. We can move mass from place to place, and transform one kind of mass into another (by a chemical reaction for example), but, just like energy, mass cannot be created nor destroyed. So both mass and energy are conserved. In fact, Einstein was able to demonstrate that all energy possesses an equivalent mass, and vice versa. To put it another way, mass and energy are really the same thing manifesting in different ways. This is the meaning of Einstein's famous equation $E=mc^2$. We can combine these principles into the conservation of mass-energy. Colloquially speaking, the amount of "stuff" in the universe is constant.

Conservation of mass-energy is exactly what we would expect on the basis of Scripture. First, the Bible indicates that no new material can come into existence. This is indicated in John 1:3 and Genesis 2:2. John 1:3 states that all things were made by God, and nothing has come into existence apart from Him. Furthermore, God ended His work of creation by the seventh day of the creation week, according to Genesis 2:2. Since only God can bring new things into existence from nothing, and since God ended His work of creation by the seventh day, no new material will come into existence today.

Second, the Bible suggests that nothing will cease to exist. This is because God is upholding all things by His sustaining power (Heb. 1:3) and by Him all things consist (Col. 1:17). Neither matter nor energy will cease to exist, because God is sustaining them, and since nothing new will come into existence, we can conclude that the amount of material in the universe is constant. Of course, the Bible makes room for miracles — supernatural interventions by God, but miracles (by definition) do not conform to the laws of physics; they are exceptions by their very nature. The universe itself obeys the law of conservation of mass-energy.

THE NUMBER OF THE STARS

The Bible often uses the "stars of heaven" to represent an extremely large quantity. Genesis 22:17 teaches that God would multiply Abraham's descendants "as the stars of the heaven, and as the sand which is on the sea shore." Genesis 32:12 makes it clear that this represents a

number which is uncountable by humans: "the sand of the sea, which cannot be numbered for multitude."[5] These are excellent analogies. Clearly the sand of the sea and the stars in the universe cannot be counted exactly by humans, though of course, they can be roughly estimated. Interestingly, the two quantities come out to about the same order of magnitude: 10^{22}, or ten billion trillion, give or take a factor of ten or so.[6]

(For other verses using stars as an illustration of large numbers, see Deuteronomy. 1:10 and 10:22.)

It was not always believed that the stars were so numerous. The astronomer Claudius Ptolemy (A.D. 150) cataloged 1,022 stars in his work *The Almagest*.[7] Many astronomers believed that these were the only stars that existed, even though Ptolemy never claimed that his catalogue was exhaustive.[8] Of course, there are many more stars than this number. The total number of stars that can be distinctly seen (from both hemispheres under ideal, dark sky conditions) with the unaided eye is around 10,000. The precise number depends on how good one's vision is.

Today, with the help of modern science, we have an even greater appreciation of just how innumerable the stars are. Powerful telescopes allow us to see stars much too distant and faint to be seen without optical aid. Even binoculars reveal countless multitudes of stars that cannot be seen by the unaided eye. It is estimated that our galaxy alone contains over 100 billion stars. Astronomers believe that there are more galaxies in the visible universe than there are stars in our own. Each of these galaxies would have hundreds of millions to trillions of stars. Modern science certainly confirms Genesis 22:17.

THE ORDINANCES OF HEAVEN AND EARTH

The Bible teaches that the universe obeys physical laws — "the ordinances of heaven and earth" (Jer. 33:25). The universe is neither haphazard nor arbitrary; nature conforms to logical, mathematical relationships set in place by the Lord.

The laws of physics and chemistry are examples of these ordinances of heaven and earth. The clockwork precision of the planets as they orbit the sun is due to their strict obedience to God's ordinances. The stars and planets are never late nor are they early. They do not fail to appear in their proper place at the proper time (Isa. 40:26).

The laws of nature are consistent and logical, because the Creator is consistent and logical. We can trust that the same physics which worked yesterday will also work today. This principle is foundational to the scientific process. The very reason that science is possible is because the universe consistently obeys simple mathematical formulae. Furthermore, God created our minds with an impressive (though finite) ability to interpret the data around us, and draw logical conclusions. We are therefore able to discover (at least to some extent) the ordinances of the universe by observation, experimentation, and logical reasoning. Once we understand the nature of these physical laws, we can use them to make accurate predictions about the future — such as computing the positions of the planets in advance.

Both earth and the rest of the physical universe ("heaven and earth") obey the laws of nature. Many ancient cultures believed that the universe beyond earth was the realm of the gods. Indeed, the planets were often worshiped as gods. In reality, the planets are simply created objects which obey the same laws of nature which we can study on earth. In an incredible leap of insight, the biblical creationist Isaac Newton realized that the moon orbits the earth because the moon is pulled by earth's gravity. The moon "falls" just like any other object; earth's gravity deflects the moon's path through space (see page 36). Since the moon has a tangential (perpendicular to the line from the earth to itself) velocity, it falls "around" the earth rather than straight down. Newton also realized that the planets orbit the sun for the same reason; the sun's gravity keeps them in their orbit. The planets and stars are not gods; they are mere creations (Gen. 1:14–19) in nature which obey the Lord's ordinances.

Creation In-Depth:

THE LAW OF GRAVITY.

Consider the law of gravitational attraction: $F = GMm/r^2$.

Here, the force of gravity (F) on an object of mass (m) produced by a nearby mass (M) at a distance (r) is related by this simple equation. The parameter (G) is the gravitational constant of the universe; it sets the overall strength of gravity. G is a very tiny number, which is why gravity is weaker than the three other known fundamental forces (electromagnetism, the weak nuclear force, and the strong nuclear force). If creation were not true — if the universe had no designer — then why should gravity obey such a simple, logical formula? For that matter, why should gravity obey any formula at all? The law of gravity suggests a law-giver; it is consistent with creation.

Of course, many of the laws of nature can be derived mathematically from other laws. For example, Kepler's laws of planetary motion can be derived from Newton's laws of gravity and motion (classical physics). And (it is thought that) the reason gravity works the way it does is because mass "curves spacetime." Essentially, space and time are treated as a "fabric" which is distorted by the presence of mass; the mass curves spacetime, and then spacetime tells the mass how to move. Many laws of nature depend on other laws which depend on still others, and so on. Ultimately, there must be a foundational set of principles which exist for no other reason than that God has so decreed. Ultimately, the fundamental laws of nature require a law-giver.

Orbit of the moon

ASTRONOMY CONFIRMS THE BIBLE

Today, the reliability of the Bible is being increasingly attacked. Can we really trust the Bible in our modern age of technology and science? As we have seen, science is not an enemy of the Bible. On the contrary, modern science has been able to confirm much of what the Bible teaches about astronomy. Many of the biblical teachings which would have been difficult to believe in the past (such as an expanding universe) are now accepted in science textbooks. This is an important lesson to learn. Ideas in secular science can change from time to time, but the Bible has demonstrated itself to be consistently true without the need for change.

Although much of secular astronomy has come to line up with the Bible, there are still a number of differences. What are we to do when the current consensus among scientists is at odds with the teachings of Scripture? Have we learned the lesson of history? Are we going to reject (or modify our "interpretation" of) the straightforward

teachings of Scripture in light of the latest secular scientific claims? Or shall we trust that the Bible will prevail again as it always has in the past?

It may help to remember that our modern age is just another point in history. Future generations (should the Lord delay His return) will no doubt look back at our time as we look back to cultures of the past. Will students in some future classroom look back with amusement at some of the "scientific" beliefs and misunderstandings of our time, the same way we smile at the scientific mistakes of ancient cultures? Will they learn about the "Great Folly" — the nearly universal belief in the big bang and molecules-to-man evolution which reigned during the 20th and early 21st centuries? Perhaps future Christians will wonder at the rampant compromise so prevalent in our time: Why did Christians of the past compromise with the secular ideas of the big bang and billions of years?

In the next chapters, we will explore points of disagreement between the straightforward teachings of the Bible and the current opinions of the majority of astronomers. If the Bible really is the Word of God, as it claims to be, then it cannot fail. Inevitably, the secular opinion will collapse, and the Bible will again be vindicated in each of these points of disagreement.

Supernova Remnant N 63A

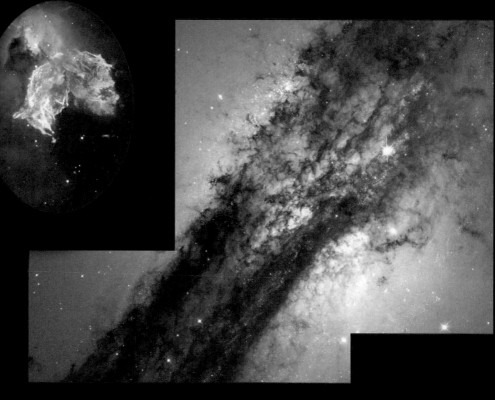

Galaxy Centaurus A (Image taken from the Hubble Space Telescope)

Trifid Nebula M20

I will surely bless you and make your
descendants as numerous as the stars in
the sky and as the sand on the seashore
(Genesis 22:17).

CHAPTER THREE

The age of the universe

The age of the universe is a point of dispute between the Bible and the opinion of the majority of astronomers today. The Bible implicitly teaches us about the age of the universe. In other words, it gives us sufficient information so that we can compute approximately how long ago God created the universe. The Bible teaches that the entire universe was created in six earth-rotation days (Exod. 20:11). Furthermore, the Bible provides the age differences between parents and descendants[9] when listing certain genealogies. From these kinds of biblical references, we know that the elapsed time between Adam and the birth of Christ was roughly 4,000 years. From other historical records, we know that Christ was born roughly 2,000 years ago. Since Adam was created on the sixth day of the creation week, we can conclude that the earth, the entire universe, and everything in it were created approximately 6,000 years ago.

Many people today would scoff at this claim. After all, most geology textbooks, astronomy textbooks, and the majority of schools and universities teach that the earth is

4.5 billion years old, and that the universe is even older, but what is the basis for the secular belief in billions of years? Why is it that so many scientists choose to ignore the recorded history of the Bible, and instead believe in a vastly inflated age of the universe?

CIRCULAR REASONING

One answer is circular reasoning: many scientists believe the world is old because they believe most other scientists think the world is old. Although a given scientist may be well aware of evidence that is not consistent with long ages, it is very tempting to dismiss such evidence because, "How could all those other scientists really be wrong?" How many of those other scientists believe in long ages simply because they also think that other scientists do? A majority opinion can become self-sustaining through circular reasoning; people believe because other people believe. It is surprising that many people do not realize the inconsistency here.

Many times, the circular reasoning can be cross-disciplinary. A geologist may feel assured that the earth is billions of years old since most astronomers believe that the solar system is billions of years old. However, an astronomer may feel confident that the solar system is billions of years old since the majority of geologists accept this for the age of the earth. Of course, the majority opinion can be wrong. In fact, many scientific discoveries have gone against the majority. Nonetheless, the psychological pressure to agree with the majority is a very powerful and well-documented phenomenon.[10]

The Evolution Connection

It is noteworthy that most (though not all) of the scientists who believe in billions of years also believe in particles-to-people evolution. Evolution requires vast ages. It couldn't possibly have happened on a mere 6,000-year time scale, because such profound changes would then have to be happening so rapidly that we would not only see massive transformations all around us, we would have historical records of many examples. Yet, we have never seen life evolve from non-life, nor have we ever seen a living organism evolve into another kind with greater specified complexity. These "uphill" changes just aren't observed; indeed, they seem to be impossible.

The imaginary vast ages are invoked to make these seemingly miraculous leaps feasible. As George Wald has stated, "Time is in fact the hero of the plot. . . . Given so much time, the 'impossible' becomes possible, the possible probable, and the probable virtually certain. One has only to wait; time itself performs the miracles."[11] The insurmountable obstacles to evolution are simply swept under the rug of vast ages.

The addition of the billions of years does not actually solve the problems with molecules-to-man evolution. These problems have been addressed in detail on our website at *answersingenesis.org* and in the materials available there, and so there is no need to elaborate in this astronomy book. The point here is simply that evolution requires vast ages. Hence, this is an example of how world views can affect a person's interpretation of evidence. Evolutionists must believe in vast ages. Their world view bias does not allow them to consider the possibility that the universe could be only thousands of years old, regardless of what recorded history teaches, and regardless of any scientific evidence. People who reject molecules-to-man evolution would do well to remember this before jumping on board with the vast ages.

Conceptual artwork of several areas of inflation (domes) in the early Universe

THE BIG-BANG CONNECTION

I have found that most people who believe in billions of years also believe in the "big-bang theory." The big bang is a secular speculation about the origin of the universe; it is an alternative to the Bible. The big bang attempts to explain the origin of the universe without God. It can be considered the cosmic equivalent of particles-to-people evolution. Sadly, a lot of Christians have bought into the idea of the big bang, without realizing that it is based on the anti-biblical philosophy of naturalism (there is no God, nature is all there is or ever was). Furthermore, they are generally not aware that the big bang contradicts the Bible on a number of points and has many scientific problems as well.

According to the big bang idea, the universe is nearly 14 billion years old; whereas the Bible indicates that the universe is about 6,000 years old. For those who claim to believe the Bible, this difference alone should be sufficient reason to reject the big bang. It is wrong about the age of the universe by a factor of over two million! But it is not just a problem of time scale; the Bible gives a different order of events than the current secular opinion. The big bang/naturalistic view teaches that stars formed before the earth, fish came about before fruit trees, and the sun came about long before plants. However, the Bible teaches the exact reverse — that the earth came before stars, fruit trees came before fish, and the plants were created before the sun.

Future of the Universe

The big bang is a story about the alleged past, but it is also a story about the alleged future. According to the currently favored version of the big bang, the universe will continue to expand indefinitely and grow colder. Usable energy will become increasingly scarce, and will eventually cease altogether, at which point the universe will die a "heat death." At this point, no "heat" will be left, so the universe will have a temperature close to absolute zero everywhere. No life will be possible at that point since no usable energy will exist.

Heat death is a rather bleak scenario, and quite different from the future the Bible teaches. Scripture indicates that the Lord will return in the future in judgment. The paradise lost in Genesis will become a paradise restored. There will be no "heat death," nor any death of humans or animals, since the Curse will be no more. The new earth will remain perfect in the Lord's presence forever. (See diagram this page.) Many Christians are inconsistent; they accept what the big bang says about the past (instead of the Bible), but reject what it says about the future (in favor of the Bible).

THE ASSUMPTIONS OF NATURALISM AND UNIFORMITARIANISM

A belief in naturalism and uniformitarianism can cause a person to make a vastly

supernaturally. The problems with naturalism will be discussed in greater detail in the next chapter. Naturalism often leads to exaggerated age estimates when applied to supernaturally created things.

As an example of this, consider the first man. Adam was created as an adult — a fully grown man. Suppose that we were asked to guess the age of Adam on the seventh day, only 24 hours after God created him. If we incorrectly assumed that Adam was not supernaturally created but that instead he came about the same way people come about today, then we would derive an age that is far too old. A naturalist might guess that the one-day-old Adam was about 30 years old by incorrectly assuming that he grew to adulthood by the same process that other people do today. Naturalism leads to an age estimate for Adam that is 10,000 times too old, but the universe was also supernaturally created. A person who denies this would likely conclude an age that is many times older than the true age.

inflated estimate of the age of the earth and universe. Recall that naturalism is the belief that nothing exists outside of nature. In this view, the universe and everything in it came about by the same kinds of processes observed within the universe. Naturalism is, of course, an unbiblical concept since the Bible makes it clear that God created the universe

Distant galaxies

A belief in uniformitarianism can also lead to severe overestimates of age. Uniformitarianism is the idea that most things in the world today (mountains and canyons, for example) were formed at about the same (i.e., uniform) rates that we see operating in the world today. People who hold to uniformitarianism would assume that radioactive decay has always occurred at the same rate, that canyons have (generally) been eroded at the same rate as today, and that mountains have been uplifted at the same average rate as today. They would certainly deny a worldwide flood (Gen. 6–8) since it would alter these rates dramatically. Uniformitari-anism can be summed up by the phrase "the present is the key to the past."[12]

However, both naturalism and uniformitarianism are merely philo-sophical assumptions. They are both anti-biblical since the Bible teaches both a supernatural creation and a worldwide flood. Moreover, naturalism and uniformitarianism can lead to con-tradictory conclusions (as we will show) which brings into question the reliability of those assumptions.

THE DISTANT STARLIGHT PROBLEM

One of the most common objections to a "young universe" is often called the "dis-tant starlight problem." There are galaxies in the universe that are incredibly far away. These distances are so extreme that even light would take billions of years to travel from these galaxies to the earth. Yet, we do see these galaxies; this indicates that the light has traveled from there to here.

Since this process is supposed to take billions of years, the universe must be at least billions of years old — much older than the biblical time scale. It is argued that distant starlight therefore supports the big-bang story of origins.

There are actually several different natural mechanisms that God might have used to get the starlight here in thousands of years. These have been published in *TJ* and other places and so we will not repeat them here. The point here is to show that the objection itself is vacuous. The argument that distant starlight disproves the biblical account of creation and supports an old "big-bang" universe is based on faulty reasoning.

First, notice that the distant starlight argument is based on the fallacious assumptions of naturalism and uniformitarianism. It assumes that the light got here entirely by natural means, and traveled at a constant rate, over a constant distance, with time also being constant. Of course, it is possible that God may indeed have used "natural

means" to get the light here. It may also be that some of the things assumed to be constant in time (such as the speed of light) are indeed constant, but is there any logical reason why we would automatically know beforehand that these must be the case? Remember that God created the lights in the sky to give light upon the earth. This happened during the creation week where God was creating in a supernatural way.

The evolutionist insists that if we cannot show a naturalistic mechanism for a particular event of the creation week (like distant starlight), then the Bible cannot be trusted. This is an unrealistic "heads I win, tails you lose" sort of argument. Since many of the events that happened during the creation week were supernatural in essence, it is irrational to demand a naturalistic explanation for them. It is ridiculous to argue that a supernatural explanation is wrong because it cannot be explained by natural causes. This would be circular reasoning. Now, it is perfectly fine to ask the question, "Did God use natural means to get

the starlight from galaxies to earth? And if so, what is the mechanism?" However, if no natural mechanism is apparent, this cannot be a legitimate criticism against supernatural creation anymore than a lack of a natural mechanism for Christ's resurrection could invalidate that event.

LIGHT TRAVEL-TIME: A PROBLEM FOR THE BIG BANG

There is another fatal flaw in using a light travel-time argument like distant starlight to reject the Bible in favor of the big bang. Such an argument is subtly self-refuting. This is because the big bang also has a light travel-time problem! In the big-bang model, light is required to travel a distance much greater than should be possible within the big bang's own time frame of about

Cosmic Microwave Background

14 billion years. This serious difficulty for the big bang is called the "horizon problem."

Creation In-depth:

THE HORIZON PROBLEM

In the big-bang model, the universe begins in an infinitely small state called a singularity, which then rapidly expands. According to the big-bang model, when the universe was still very small it would have developed different temperatures in different locations. (See illustration opposite page.) Let's suppose that point A is hot and point B is cold. Today, the universe has expanded and points A and B are now widely separated.

However, the universe has an extremely uniform temperature at great distance — beyond the farthest known galaxies. In other words, points A and B have almost exactly the same temperature today. We know this because we see electromagnetic

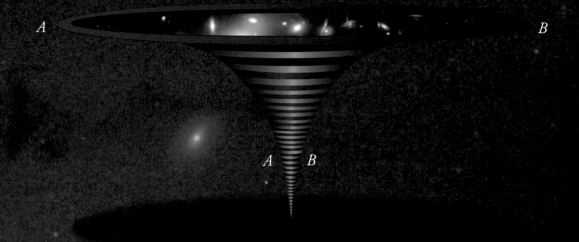

radiation coming from all directions in space in the form of microwaves. This is called the "cosmic microwave background" (CMB). The frequencies of radiation have a characteristic temperature of 2.7 K and are extremely uniform in all directions. The temperature deviates by only one part in 10^5.

The problem is this: how did points A and B come to be the same temperature? They can only do this by exchanging energy. There are many systems where this happens; consider an ice cube placed in hot coffee. The ice heats up and the coffee cools down by exchanging energy. Likewise, point A can give energy to point B

in the form of electromagnetic radiation (light). (This is the fastest way of transferring energy since nothing can travel faster than light.) However, using the big-bang supporters' own assumptions (such as uniformitarianism and naturalism), there has not been enough time in 14 billion years to get light from A to B; they are too far apart. This is a light travel-time problem — and a very serious one. After all, A and B have almost the same temperature today, and so must have exchanged light multiple times.

Big-bang supporters have proposed a number of conjectures which attempt to solve the big bang's light travel-time problem. One of the most popular is called "inflation." In "inflationary" models, the universe has two expansion rates; a normal rate and a fast "inflation" rate. The universe begins with the "normal" rate (which is actually quite rapid, but is slow by comparison to the next phase). Then it enters the inflation phase, where the universe expands much more rapidly. At a later time, the universe goes back to the normal rate. This all happens early on, long before stars and galaxies form.

The inflation model allows points A and B to exchange energy (during the first normal expansion) and to then be pushed apart during the inflation phase to the enormous distances at which they are located today, but the inflation model amounts to nothing more than storytelling, with no supporting evidence at all. It is merely a speculation designed to align the big bang to conflicting observations. Moreover, inflation adds an additional set of problems and difficulties to the big-bang model, such as what would

cause such inflation, and how to turn it off in a graceful fashion. An increasing number of secular astrophysicists are rejecting inflation for these reasons and others. Clearly, the horizon problem remains a serious light travel-time problem for the big bang.

The critic may suggest that the big bang is a better explanation of origins than the Bible since biblical creation has a light travel-time problem — distant starlight. Such an argument is not rational since the big bang has a light travel-time problem of its own. If both models have the same problem in essence,[13] then that problem cannot be used to support one model over the other. Therefore, distant starlight cannot be used to dismiss the Bible in favor of the big bang.

ATTEMPTS AT COMPROMISE

The belief in billions of years has a stranglehold on our culture today — even within the church. Many professing Christians have been taken in by the fallacious distant starlight argument or other eisegetical[14] claims involving anti-biblical assumptions. As a result, many Christians have compromised; they have attempted to "add" the billions of years to the Bible. One of the most common methods of trying to believe both the Bible and the billions of years is called the "day-age" position. In this view, the days of creation were not actually days, but rather were vast ages — many millions of years each. According to the day-age idea, God created over six long periods of time.

It is important to point out that even if the day-age position were true, it would not bring the biblical account into alignment with the secular story of origins since the order of events is different between the two. Recall that the big bang/naturalism view teaches that stars existed long before fruit trees, which came after fish. The Bible teaches that fish were made on day 5 after the stars which were made on day 4, and after the trees which were made on day 3 — regardless of how long the days were.

Day-age followers point out that the Hebrew word for day (yom) does not always indicate a "day" in the ordinary sense, but can sometimes mean an unspecified period of time. In certain contexts, "day" can refer to a longer period of time, but not in the context of the days of creation. Similarly, our English word "day" can mean an unspecified period of time in certain contexts like "back in grandfather's day. . . ." However, it would not mean an unspecified period of time in other contexts such as "five days ago, the third day, day then night, morning of the day, evening of the day, the evening and

morning."

Clearly, in the preceding phrases the word "day" must mean an ordinary day from context — not a period of time.

The Hebrew language also obeys grammatical rules, and as with English, the meaning of a word is always determined by its context. The Hebrew word for day means an ordinary day (and is never translated as "time") when in any of the following contexts:

(1) When combined with an ordinal (list) number ("the first day, the third day, etc.") day means an ordinary day — not a period of time.

(2) When associated with the word "morning," such as "There was morning that day," day means an ordinary day — not a period of time.

(3) When associated with the word "evening," such as "There was evening that day," day means an ordinary day — not a period of time.

(4) When evening and morning occur together, such as "There was evening and morning" (even if the word "day" is not present), this constitutes an ordinary day — not a nonspecific period of time.

(5) When contrasted with "night," such as "There was night then day," the word day means an ordinary day — not a period of time.

In Genesis chapter 1, we see all of these contextual indicators used for the days

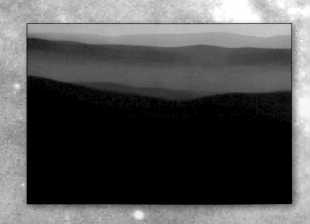

of creation. The days of creation must be ordinary days from context; they cannot be long periods of time because context does not permit this. It would be wrong to try and read "day" to mean "a period of time" in Genesis 1, when the context clearly precludes such a meaning; such an error is called an unwarranted expansion of an expanded semantic field. The day-age idea is not logically sound; it is simply an unsuccessful attempt to make the Bible compatible with anti-biblical notions.[15]

Ultimately, the Bible teaches that God created in six days and the secular opinion is that the universe evolved over billions of years. Each of us must decide whether we are going to trust the secular opinions of human beings, or the clear teaching of the Bible. As we saw in the last chapter, the Bible has always been correct when it touches upon astronomy.

It is important to remember that we are at just another point in history. Yes, people today will scoff at and ridicule a belief in a "young universe." Then again, many of those same people will ridicule a belief in Jesus Christ being the one true God, or even the very belief in a Creator. The Bible has always been vindicated in the past. So there is no reason to cave in to mere peer pressure today.

THE EVIDENCE CONFIRMS A YOUNG UNIVERSE

Even now, the scientific evidence is very consistent with what the Bible teaches about the age of the universe. Why then do many secular scientists believe that the evidence points to a multi-billion-year-old universe? People who believe in the big bang generally interpret the evidence according to the big bang (sometimes without even realizing it). In other words, they simply assume that the big bang is true and they interpret the evidence to match their beliefs. We all interpret the evidence in light of our world view; there is no getting around it. However,

the Bible can also be used to interpret the evidence. Since the Bible records the true history of the universe, we will see that it makes a lot more sense of the evidence than the big bang does. Let us now look at some facts about the universe. We will see that the evidence is consistent with 6,000 years, but

doesn't make as much sense if we hold to the big bang.

Of course, big-bang supporters can always reinterpret the evidence by adding on extra assumptions, so, these facts that follow are not intended to "prove" that the Bible is right about the age of the universe. The Bible is right in all matters because it is the Word of God. However, when we understand the scientific evidence, we will find that it agrees with what the Bible teaches. The evidence is certainly consistent with a "young" (roughly 6,000-year-old) universe.

RECESSION OF THE MOON

As the moon orbits the earth, its gravity pulls on the earth's oceans, causing tides. Since the earth rotates faster than the moon orbits, the tidal bulges induced by the moon are always "ahead" of the moon. For this reason the tides actually "pull forward" on the moon, which causes the moon to gain energy and gradually spiral outward. The moon moves about an inch and a half farther away from the earth every year due to this tidal interaction. Thus, the moon would have been closer to the earth in the past.

Six thousand years ago, the moon would have been about 800

feet (250 m) closer to the earth (which is not much of a change considering the moon is nearly a quarter of a million miles, or 400,000 km, away). So this "spiraling away" of the moon is not a problem over the biblical time scale of 6,000 years, but if the earth and moon were over 4,000,000,000 years old (as big-bang supporters teach), then we would have big problems. This is because the moon would have been so close that it would actually have been touching the

earth less than 1.5 billion years ago. This suggests that the moon can't possibly be as old as secular astronomers claim.

Secular astronomers who assume the big bang is true must invoke other explanations to get around this. For example, they might assume that the rate at which the moon was receding was actually smaller in the past (for whatever reason), but this is an extra assumption needed to make their billions-of-years model work.

The simplest explanation is that the moon hasn't been around for that long. The recession of the moon is a problem for a belief in billions of years, but is perfectly consistent with a young age.

Creation In-depth:

RECESSION OF THE MOON

Tidal bulges develop on earth because the moon is closer to one side of the earth than the other, and thus its gravity pulls harder on the near side. This causes the overall shape of the earth to be slightly elliptical. The height of the tidal bulges would be greater if the moon were closer to the earth. The earth rotates faster than the moon revolves; thus, the tidal bulges are always ahead of the moon. Since they pull forward on the moon, the bulges transfer angular momentum and kinetic energy — increasing the moon's orbital energy and causing it to move away from the earth. The rate of this recession is approximately proportional to the inverse sixth power of the earth-moon distance. As a rough estimation, this can be shown as follows:

The tidal bulges are approximated as a dipole (two points separated from the center of the earth). The dipole separation is proportional to $1/r^3$, where r is the earth-moon separation.[16] So, we would expect that tidal bulge height goes as roughly $h=1/r^3$. However, the force with which the tidal bulges pull back on the moon also goes as h/r^3 for a given height (h). So we expect the rate of tidal recession goes as approximately $1/r^6$.

It follows that the equation describing tidal recession is:

$$dr/dt = k/r^6$$

The constant k can be found using the current measured rate of lunar recession: 3.8 cm/year. Thus, $k = r^6 dr/dt = (384,401km)^6 \times (.000038km/year) = 1.2 \times 10^{29}$ km^7/year. The lunar recession equation is then solved for the extreme case (the upper limit on age of the moon):

$$dt = (r^6/k)dr$$

$$\int_0^T dt = \int_0^R (r^6/k)dr$$

$$T = R^7/(7k)$$

Here, T is the maximum age for the moon since this assumes it migrated from a distance of zero to its current distance of R = 384,401 km. Plugging in the known values gives an upper limit on the age of the earth-moon system of T = 1.5 billion years — much less than the 4.5 billion years that evolutionists require.

Since critics of biblical creation cannot accept this conclusion, they are forced to adopt secondary assumptions to make the evidence fit. Some have suggested that k may not be constant in time; perhaps the different distribution of continents in the past affected the tidal breaking of the earth's oceans. This speculation does not necessarily solve the problem though. First, a different continental distribution does not guarantee that k would be smaller; if it were larger, then the problem would be even worse.

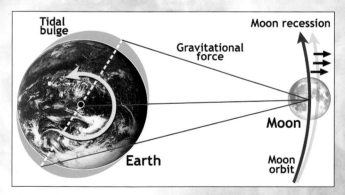

Tidal bulge
Gravitational force
Moon recession
Earth
Moon
Moon orbit

Second, k would have to be substantially smaller in order to ameliorate the problem. Third, geological evidence argues against this claim, even if we accept the evolutionary/long-age interpretation of such evidence. Studies of tidal rhythmites performed by secular scientists are consistent with k being approximately constant over geologic time (assuming the evolutionists' dating methods).[17] Furthermore, there is no evidence of the extreme tides that would have resulted from a moon that is very close to the earth.[18] Of course, this is what biblical creationists would expect, since the moon was only about 800 feet (250 m) closer at creation, roughly 6,000 years ago.

THE MAGNETIC FIELD OF THE EARTH

Most people have some familiarity with magnets, like the kind that stick to a refrigerator door. Magnets have an almost "magical" ability to attract other magnets or certain metals separated by a distance — they seem to reach out over space and pull with invisible fingers. The region of space surrounding a magnet which exerts a force on other magnets is called a "magnetic field." Magnetic fields are caused by electric current — motion of charged particles.[19]

The earth's magnetic field is approximated by a "dipole" — meaning the magnet has one north pole and one south pole (see opposite page, below). This dipole is roughly aligned with the earth's rotation axis (being off by about 11.5 degrees). That is, the north magnetic pole is close to the north rotation pole. This is why a compass points approximately north; it aligns with the geomagnetic field. This magnetic

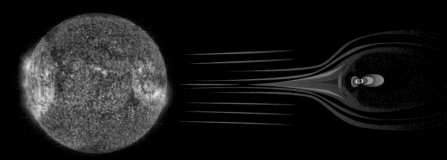

The earth's magnetic field

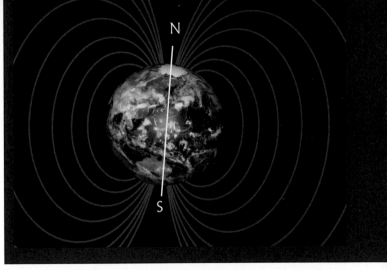

field surrounds the earth and is an important design feature. The universe contains radiation which is harmful to living tissue. Earth's magnetic field protects life by deflecting dangerous cosmic radiation. The atmosphere also offers some protection.

The earth's magnetic field is caused by electric currents within its interior. Such currents encounter electrical resistance, and so they naturally decay with time. We would therefore expect that earth's magnetic field would become weaker as time progresses. We have been able to measure the strength of the magnetic field for over a century, and not surprisingly, the earth's mag-

netic field is indeed decaying. Every century, the magnetic field decays by about 5 percent. Since the earth's magnetic field gets weaker as time moves forward, it must have been considerably stronger in the past. Approximately 6,000 years ago, the magnetic field would have been quite a lot stronger, but still perfectly suitable for life. However, if the earth were many millions of years old, then the geomagnetic field would have been so strong in that alleged distant past, that life would not have been possible.[20]

has not decreased. However, this is not the case; any increase in the non-dipole field has been shown to be much smaller than the decrease in the dipole field.[21] Thus, the total energy of the earth's magnetic field is decaying and therefore supports a recent creation.

Creation In-depth:

GETTING AROUND THE MAGNETIC FIELD EVIDENCE

The straightforward interpretation that the earth is not billions of years old is, of course, an intolerable conclusion for evolutionists. Additional assumptions are therefore required to explain this evidence within the naturalist's world view. So far, however, the secular explanations have not been able to endure careful scrutiny. For example, some secular scientists have suggested that only the dipole component of earth's magnetic field has been decaying, and that the non-dipole components have increased in energy to compensate. They've suggested that the overall energy of earth's magnetic field

MAGNETIC FIELDS OF THE PLANETS

Many of the planets of the solar system also have strong dipole magnetic fields. Jupiter's magnetic field, for example, is extremely powerful. The magnetic fields of Uranus and Neptune are also quite strong. If these planets were really billions of years old (as secular astronomers believe), their magnetic fields should be extremely weak by now. Yet, they are not. A reasonable explanation for this is that these planets are only a few thousand years old, as the Bible teaches.

The suggestion that the solar system is only thousands of years old is, of course, an

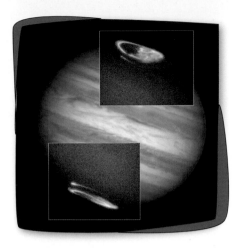

Jupiter's aurora

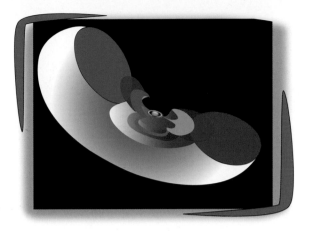

Saturn's magnetic field

intolerable position for those who believe in particles-to-people evolution. The vast ages are required for their world view, and so must be protected at all costs. Therefore, the apparent youth of the universe must be explained away by the addition of auxiliary hypotheses. For example, secular astronomers have proposed that planetary magnetic fields can be "recharged" over time. Specifically, they invoke the idea of a "magnetic dynamo" powering the magnetic fields of of planets. The basic idea is that motion within the planets can regener-the magnetic fields so that the total field strength will not decay.

However, the planets do not fit the conditions necessary to drive such a dynamo. The simplest explanation is that the solar system is much younger than billions of years.

Creation In-depth:

MAGNETIC DYNAMO VERSUS MAGNETIC DECAY.

Magnetic and electrical energy can be generated from mechanical energy (motion). This is how the alternator in a car works. Undoubtedly, there are places in the universe where mechanical energy is converted into magnetic fields. It seems likely that the sun undergoes just such a process; it reverses its magnetic field every 11 years. Many secular astronomers assume that the planets also undergo such a process (though this has not been observed in the present). However, the fact that such processes can occur (and there is good evidence for magnetic reversals preserved in earth rocks, for which there is a respectable creationist theory[22]) does not necessarily solve the problem of strong magnetic fields for an "old" universe.

First, an electromagnetic-mechanical system must be set up in just the right way in order to cause the total magnetic field energy to increase. There is no guarantee that vigorous motions which cause magnetic field reversals could actually recharge the total magnetic field energy and prevent it from decaying with time. In fact, such magnetic field reversals might actually accelerate the decay of the total field strength — as may be the case with the sun.[23]

Second, there are a number of good reasons to believe that the magnetic fields of the planets are not dynamos, and are much different than that of the sun. The sun is so hot that most of its atoms are ionized — the electrons have been stripped away from the nucleus in a state called "plasma." Plasma is highly sensitive to magnetic fields, and interacts with them much more strongly than neutral gas. The turbulent motions within the sun are constantly generating chaotic bits of magnetism. However, the planets are not made of plasma and do not exhibit the kinds of motions we see in the sun. Additionally, in the process by which the sun is thought to reverse its magnetic field, the rotation axis should be almost exactly aligned with the magnetic poles. This is the case for the sun, but not for the planets. In fact, the planets Uranus and Neptune have magnetic fields which are tilted severely relative to their respective rotation axes.

The sun also possesses powerful toroidal magnetic fields (in addition to a dipole field). Instead of having a north and south magnetic pole, toroidal magnetic fields make a complete loop around the sun, forming bands parallel to the solar equator. At least one band exists in the Northern Hemisphere, and another is in the Southern Hemisphere with opposite polarity. Sunspots generally occur at the latitudes of these toroidal bands. These toroidal magnetic fields are critical in the process of reversing the sun's magnetic field, and yet the planets do not show evidence of strong toroidal magnetic fields. Moreover, there is no evidence that the magnetic fields of the planets are reversing today as the sun's does.[24] The magnetic fields of the planets today are consistent with the simple decay produced by electrical resistance.

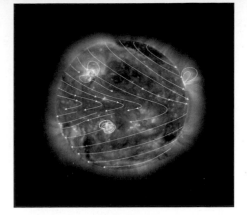

The sun's magnetic field

MAGNETIC FIELDS CONFIRM RECENT CREATION

Dr. Russ Humphreys, (a Ph.D. physicist and biblical creationist) has produced a model of planetary magnetic fields which can explain their present strengths in terms of biblical creation.[25] In essence, the model estimates the initial strength of each magnetic field at the moment of its creation, then the model computes their present strengths based on 6,000 years of decay from electrical resistance. Impressively, this biblically based model is able to account for the present measured magnetic fields of all the known planets[26] and even many of the moons as well.

Of course, almost any model can be "adjusted" to fit existing data, so it is perhaps even more impressive that Dr. Humphreys' model successfully predicted the present magnetic field strengths of the planets Uranus and Neptune before they were measured by the Voyager spacecraft. Specific, successful predictions are the mark of a good scientific model. Dr. Humphreys also predicted that Mars would have remanent (permanent) magnetism, which has now been confirmed.[27] Remanent magnetism occurs in rocks which cooled and solidified in the presence of an external magnetic field. Such remanent magnetism is also found on the moon. This confirms that both the moon and Mars once had strong magnetic fields as expected in the Humphreys model. Planetary magnetic fields strongly support the biblical age of the solar system.

Creation In-depth:

DR. HUMPHREYS' MODEL OF PLANETARY MAGNETIC FIELDS

Dr. Russ Humphreys has produced a creation-based model of planetary magnetic fields. This model proposes that when God created the planets of the solar system, He made them first as water which God then supernaturally changed into the substances of which the planets are comprised today. This idea may be suggested (at least for the earth) in passages such as 2 Peter 3:5. Water molecules can have a small magnetic field of their own due to the quantum spin of the proton in each of the two hydrogen atoms. If a significant fraction of these molecular magnetic fields were aligned when the planets were first created, they would add to produce a strong dipole magnetic field. Although the molecular alignment would quickly cease due to random thermal motion of the molecules, the magnetic field would induce electric currents which would maintain the strength of the magnetic field.

After God transforms the water into other materials, the electric current maintaining the magnetic field will begin to decay as it encounters electrical resistance within the material. The greater the electrical conductivity of the material, the longer it will take for the magnetic field to decay. To compute the current magnetic field of any given planet, we simply need to know the initial magnetic field strength of the planet, and then reduce this by the decay after 6,000 years. This is determined by (1) the amount of alignment (k) of the original magnetic fields, and (2) the size of the planet's conductive core. A larger, more conductive core will allow electric currents to last longer; thus, the magnetic field will take longer to decay.

The mass of each of the planets is well known and can be computed very precisely from the periods of any orbiting moons (or the trajectories of nearby space probes). The core size and conductivity can be estimated as well. The only free parameter of the model is the amount of initial alignment which could be between k=0 (no molecular alignment) and k=1 (maximum alignment). Dr. Humphreys now thinks that the data are most consistent with k=1. Using such a value, the earth's present magnetic field is perfectly consistent with this model. Furthermore, since k cannot be greater than 1, this sets an absolute upper limit on all the magnetic fields of the sun and planets today. Indeed, none of the known magnetic fields in the solar system exceeds the upper limit predictions based on this model, yet the evidence is compelling that they would have been reasonably close to this limit at their creation roughly 6,000 years ago. The evidence fits very well with the biblical time scale.

SPIRAL GALAXIES

A galaxy is an enormous assembly of stars and interstellar gas and dust. Galaxies occur in a range of sizes and can contain anywhere from a million to a trillion stars.

Our galaxy (the Milky Way) contains over 100 billion stars. Galaxies also come in a range of shapes. Many are round or elliptical in nature. Others have an irregular shape, such as the clouds of Magellan — two satellite galaxies of the Milky Way. Some of the most beautiful galaxies are spiral in nature. A spiral galaxy has a flat-disk shape with a central bulge. The disk section contains spiral arms — regions with greater numbers of stars which extend from the periphery of the galaxy to the core.

Spiral galaxies slowly rotate, but the inner regions of the spiral rotate faster than the outer regions; this is called "differential rotation." This means that a spiral galaxy is constantly becoming more and more twisted up as the spiral becomes tighter. After a few hundred million years, the galaxy would be wound so tightly that the spiral structure would no longer be recognizable. According to the big-bang scenario, galaxies are supposed to be many billions of years old,

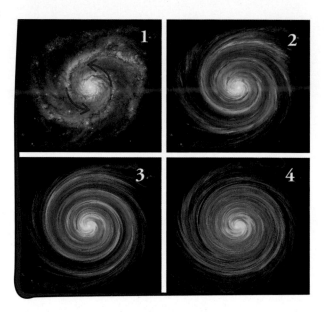

Differential rotation of a Spiral galaxy

yet we do see spiral galaxies — and lots of them. This suggests that they are not nearly as old as the big bang requires. Spiral galaxies are consistent with the biblical age of the universe, but are problematic for a belief in billions of years.

Secular astronomers have proposed "spiral density waves" to create new spiral arms as old ones become twisted beyond recognition. The idea is that waves of pressure travel around the galaxy and stimulate new star growth. Of course, such waves have not been observed, so the idea remains a conjecture. Furthermore, the spiral density wave notion assumes that stars can form spontaneously. Although virtually all secular astronomers assume this, star formation has significant problems of its own. Furthermore, there are difficulties in starting any supposed density wave in the first place. Such complications are not necessary if we accept the most straightforward interpretation of the evidence: galaxies are not billions of years old.

COMETS

Comets are balls of ice and dirt which orbit the sun, often in highly eccentric orbits. The solid central portion of a comet is called the nucleus. Comets generally have a region of vaporized material surrounding them which appears as a faint "fog" — this is called the "coma." Comets spend most of their time moving slowly near the point in their orbit that is farthest from the sun (aphelion). As they approach the sun, they speed up and slingshot around the sun, mov-

ing fastest at the closest point (perihelion). It is during these points of close approach that many comets develop a "tail" — a stream of vaporized material which extends away from the comet. The tail points away from the sun, because the material is swept away by solar wind and radiation. Often two tails develop: an ion tail consisting of light charged particles, and a dust tail containing heavier materials. The ion tail is slightly blue in color; it is straight and points directly away from the sun. The dust tail is white and is generally curved. Sometimes only one of the two tails is visible.

Interior view of a comet.

Hale-Bopp comet

the Bible. Clearly, 4.5 billion years would be an absurdly inflated age for comets.

How do secular astronomers attempt to reconcile this with their belief in billions of years? Since comets can't last that long, secular astronomers must assume that new comets are introduced to the solar system to replace those that are gone, so they've invented the idea of an "Oort cloud."[29] This is supposed to be a vast reservoir of icy masses orbiting far away from the sun. The idea is that occasionally an icy mass falls into the inner solar system to become a "new" comet. It is interesting that there is currently no evidence of an Oort cloud, and there is no reason to believe in one if we accept the creation account in Genesis. Comets are consistent with the fact that the solar system is young.

A comet's tail (or tails) is an indication that comets cannot last forever. The tail means that the comet is losing material; a comet gets smaller every time it orbits the sun. It has been estimated that a typical comet can only orbit the sun for about 100,000 years at most before completely running out of material. (This is an average figure, of course; the exact life span would depend on how big the comet is to begin with, and the parameters of its orbit.) Since we still have a lot of comets, this suggests that the solar system is much younger than 100,000 years. This agrees perfectly with

CONCLUSIONS

Clearly, there are many evidences which are fully consistent with the biblical age of the universe and are difficult to reconcile with a belief in billions of years. They are not "proofs," since big-bang supporters can

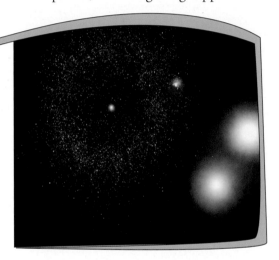

Artist rendition of the (purely hypothetical) Oort cloud as seen from the Alpha Centuri system

always invent non-falsifiable conjectures to explain away these evidences, but we have seen that when we use the Bible to understand the age of the universe, the evidence is certainly consistent.

In most of the arguments for a young universe discussed above, we have used uniformitarian and naturalistic assumptions, which of course we do not accept. We have deliberately used the assumptions of the opposing point of view to show that these assumptions lead to contradictions. For example, we showed that assuming that the moon formed naturalistically 4.5 billion years ago, and that the rate of spiraling away hasn't deviated (from the constant $1/r^6$ relation) then the moon can't be older than 1.5 billion years — a contradiction. Such inconsistencies are common in non-biblical world views.

Uniformitarianism is a blind philosophical assumption; it is not a conclusion based on evidence. Furthermore, it is incompatible with the Bible. The present is not the key to the past. Just the opposite: the past is the key to the present! The Bible is the revealed Word of the Creator God who knows everything, and has given us an accurate account of history. The Bible (which tells us about the past) is the key to understanding the present world. When we start with the Bible as our presupposition, we find that it makes sense of the world. Of course the planets would have strong magnetic fields; of course galaxies would not be twisted up; and of course we still have comets. These are what we would expect in a biblical world view. The Bible is true, and the evidence confirms that the universe is thousands of years old.

Orion Nebula

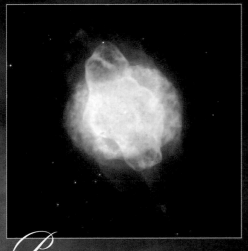

$\mathcal{P}$lanetary Nebula NGC 3918 is in the constellation Centaurus and is about 3,000 light-years from us. Its diameter is about 0.3 light-years. It shows a roughly spherical outer envelope but an elongated inner balloon inflated by a fast wind from the hot central star, which is starting to break out of the spherical envelope at the top and bottom of the image.

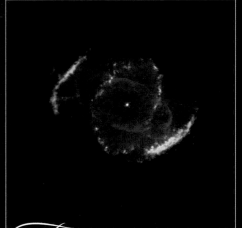

$\mathcal{T}$his NASA Hubble Space Telescope image shows one of the most complex planetary nebulae ever seen, NGC 6543, nicknamed the "Cat's Eye Nebula." Hubble reveals surprisingly intricate structures including concentric gas shells, jets of high-speed gas and unusual shock-induced knots of gas.

This Hubble image of the "Red Rectangle" nebula reveals strange step-like features. The nebula is the result of hydrogen gas being ejected from the central star.

Planetary nebula NGC 6853

A close-up portion of the Dumbbell Nebula reveals fine, wispy clouds of hydrogen gas. This planetary nebula lies in the constellation Vulpecula, and can be seen with a small telescope on a dark summer night.

CHAPTER FOUR

The Bible and modern astronomy

Aside from the issue of the age of the universe, there are several other matters where the majority of astronomers today disagree with a straightforward reading of the Bible. In this chapter, we will investigate these differences, and we will see that the evidence very much supports the Genesis record of creation. We will explore the concept of naturalism and examine the philosophic and scientific problems with it. We will examine the question of the uniqueness of the earth and the concept of extraterrestrial "alien" life.

NATURALISM VERSUS SUPERNATURALISM

Perhaps the most obvious difference between the biblical view and the secular view lies in the first verse of the Bible, "In the beginning God created. . . ." This stands in stark contrast to the secular teaching of a universe which spontaneously formed in a big bang. The big bang, and secular ideas about the formation of galaxies, the solar system, etc. are naturalistic explanations of origins. They are atheistic in nature. This is not to say that everyone who holds these views is necessarily an atheist, but these naturalistic formation scenarios attempt to explain the creation of the universe and things within it (galaxies, stars, planets, etc.) without God. None of the astronomy textbooks I have used in my undergraduate education or doctoral program give credit to God for the creation of the universe or anything within it. All events are described in terms of what can be explained within the laws of nature — nothing beyond nature is allowed. This is naturalism.

The Bible is supernaturalistic. The Bible makes it clear that God (either directly or indirectly) made everything that was made (John 1:3). God is "outside" of the physical universe; He is not bound by it. The Christian world view is therefore supernatural in nature. The Christian claims that the processes which created the universe are not the processes that exist within it.

THE PHILOSOPHY OF NATURALISM

Naturalism is extremely popular in scientific circles today. In fact, many scientists even equate science with naturalism.

After all, science depends on the fact that there are laws of nature which the universe consistently obeys. Take gravity, for example. If I drop a pen, I know it will fall down at a given acceleration because of the well-known law of gravity. A naturalist might argue that if there is a God who constantly intervenes (by, for example, making my pen float, or fall up, etc.), then how would we ever learn about gravity? Experimentation would be pointless since we might get a different result every time. We would never know if we were learning something about the universe, or witnessing a miracle. Therefore, the naturalist concludes, science requires naturalism.

This kind of argument might be a reasonable objection to a haphazard god who is inconsistent and whimsical. However, this is not the biblical God. The God of Scripture does not arbitrarily suspend the laws of nature which He created. Certainly

Christ Walks on Water

God can bend, change, suspend, or reverse the laws of nature — and has done so on special occasions for special purposes (for example, Christ's walking on the water, and the Resurrection itself). The laws of nature were created by God and depend on God's sustaining power for their continued existence (Heb. 1:3). Clearly God is not "bound" by them, as we are. Many of the miracles recorded in the Bible seem to be

Resurrection of Christ

special cases where God has worked outside the "normal" operation of the universe. However, these miracles are (by definition) exceptions and therefore rare. Primarily, the Lord accomplishes His will by upholding the laws of nature which He created, not by suspending them. Another way of putting it might be that the operation of "natural law" is God's normative way of working.

Both the Christian and the naturalist agree that there are laws of nature which the universe "obeys" (i.e., which describe the consistent, predictable behavior of things) and that scientific experimentation can be used to probe these laws. Therefore, it is indeed possible to study and understand the universe in the Christian world view. In fact, Christianity provides the basis for such scientific research.

The Christian expects the universe to obey laws because God created those laws — the "ordinances of heaven and earth" (Jer. 33:25). The creationist expects that the laws of nature that applied yesterday will apply in the future as well; this is because God is consistent (Mal. 3:6) and does not arbitrarily change His mind (Num. 23:19). We expect the universe to be understandable, because God created it and He created us with the ability to reason (Isa. 1:18) and understand. However, the naturalist cannot account for these properties of the universe. What reason does he have for expecting the universe to be consistent and predictable? Why should a naturalist be able to assume that the same laws that apply here on earth also apply on, for example, the surface of the star Alpha Centauri? Applying such assumptions has been overwhelmingly successful, but they are not assumptions that arise out of naturalism, but from the Bible.

So, the objection that science and knowledge are impossible without a belief in naturalism actually backfires on the naturalist. If the universe had not been designed by God, then why should it obey any laws of nature? Where did the laws of nature come from, and why do they obey logical mathematical relationships? If our brains are merely the result of a random sequence of accidental mutations, then why should we think that they can determine truth? A brain is merely a collection of electrochemical interactions which conveyed some sort of survival value in our past — in the secular scenario. There is no reason to think we can reason if naturalism were true, so we see that the naturalist is unable to account for science and knowledge within his own world view. He must borrow creationist ideas (that laws of nature exist and are understandable, etc.) in order to do science.

It is also crucial to point out that the origin of the universe is a different issue from the current operation of the universe. The naturalist blindly assumes that the universe was caused by the kinds of processes we see operating within the universe today.[30] Of course, there is no logically compelling reason to believe this, and it would be absurd to assume that this necessarily applies to anything else. For example, a telescope operates by reflecting and refracting light to a focal point, but the telescope was not created by this process.

The Bible makes it abundantly clear that the universe was supernaturally created by God. Genesis 1 specifically lists a number of astronomical objects which were made by the Lord; He made the heavens,[31] the earth (Gen. 1:1), the sun, the moon, and the stars also (Gen. 1:14–16). This means that galaxies were created supernaturally (since they are comprised of stars), and the other planets are as well (since planets are "stars" in the biblical nomenclature[32]). These things were supernaturally created, and therefore seeking a naturalistic explanation for them (as many secular astronomers do) is an exercise in futility. We would therefore expect some scientific problems in the naturalistic explanations for the origins of stars, the planets, and the

Earth, the moon, and the sun

universe, and this is exactly what we find.

A FEW SCIENTIFIC DIFFICULTIES FOR NATURALISTS

Since secular ideas of the origin of the universe are based on a faulty premise (naturalism), they abound with scientific problems and inconsistencies. An exhaustive discussion of the scientific problems with naturalistic ideas on the origin and evolution of the universe, stars, and planets would take volumes. Let us examine just a few of these.

Regarding the (big-bang) naturalistic attempt to explain the origin of the universe, there is a serious issue called the baryon number problem — the problem of the missing antimatter (see in-depth box). Stated concisely, if the big bang were true, it should have produced antimatter (a substance like ordinary matter but with the charges of the particles reversed). In fact there should be as much antimatter in the universe as ordinary matter — yet there is virtually none. This is a fatal problem for the big bang. The almost complete absence of antimatter in the universe testifies to its supernatural origin.

WHERE'S THE ANTIMATTER?

One of the many scientific problems with the big–bang notion is called the "baryon number problem." In the big-bang scenario, the universe starts out infinitely small, and infinitely hot, in a point called a "singularity." All the energy in the universe, and even "space itself," is contained in this point. The point rapidly expands like a balloon and the energy cools as it is dispersed. The energy forms matter — hydrogen and helium gas. It is this gas which allegedly condenses to form stars and galaxies. Virtually every step in this conjectured process is riddled with problems that are indicative of the big bang's dismal inadequacy as a scientific model.[33] Let's highlight one of these problems involving the conversion of energy to matter.

Energy can indeed be transformed into matter. This can be done in a laboratory. However, such reactions always produce an equal amount of a substance called "antimatter." Each class of particle of matter has a corresponding anti-particle. Antimatter is identical to ordinary matter in virtually all respects except one: the charge of the particle is reversed. So, whereas a proton has a positive electrical charge, its antimatter counterpart, the "anti-proton," has a negative charge. Likewise, electrons are negatively charged, but an anti-electron (also called a "positron") has a positive charge. As far as we know, it is impossible to create matter from energy without creating an exactly equal amount of anti-matter. This is what laboratory science has shown us.

If the big bang had actually happened, it too would have produced an equal amount of antimatter. Therefore, the universe today should have an equal amount of matter and antimatter. But it doesn't. The universe is made almost entirely of matter. This is no slight imbalance; it is a huge problem. It is estimated that the universe contains 10^{80} atoms (that's a one followed by 80 zeros). Each of these has a nucleus made of protons (and sometimes neutrons). Protons and neutrons are "baryons." There are ubiquitous baryons in the universe, and yet there are virtually no anti-baryons to be found!

Big-bang supporters have come up with an idea to try and save the big bang from this baryon number problem. They have proposed that on extremely rare occasions energy can produce matter only — with no antimatter produced as a byproduct. Indeed, there are a number of variant speculations in physics that rely on this notion to solve the problem of the missing antimatter, but, of course, this idea does not rely on the results of observational science. Observations have shown that matter and antimatter are always produced in pairs; we have never seen one produced without the other. As usual, the naturalist must rely on conjectures that are inconsistent with observations. The baryon number problem remains a serious defect

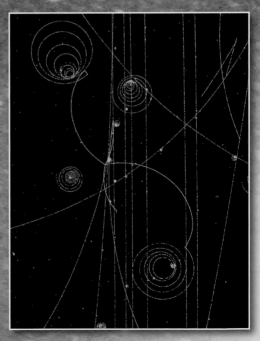

Sub-atomic particle tracks

in the big-bang model.

This problem for the big bang is actually a design feature for biblical creation. When particles and anti-particles touch, they destroy each other and release enormous amounts of energy. If God had made the universe with equal amounts of matter and antimatter (as physics requires for a natural origin), then the matter in the universe would have been destroyed by any contact with antimatter, releasing devastating amounts of dangerous radiation. The universe contains virtually matter only because it was supernaturally designed and created by God.

SOLAR SYSTEM

FORMA- TION

Secular models of solar system formation have also come up short. The earth, moon, sun, and all the planets have supposedly formed from a collapsing nebula — a cloud of hydrogen and helium gas. The model is upheld by secular astronomers because it can account for some of the properties of the solar system. One such property is the fact that the small rocky worlds (Mercury, Venus, Earth, and Mars) orbit close to the sun, whereas the giant gas planets (Jupiter, Saturn, Uranus, and Neptune) orbit farther away (see creation in-depth box). This was therefore expected to be a general trend of solar systems. Thus, planets orbiting other stars can serve as test cases for the standard model of solar system formation.

We have now discovered over 150 planets orbiting other stars. Contrary to the expectations of the secular model of solar system formation, most of these extra-solar planets are large giant gas worlds that orbit very close to their star — in many cases closer than Mercury orbits the sun. This is a devastating blow to secular solar system formation scenarios. However, the diversity of these solar systems is consistent with the creative variety God has demonstrated throughout the cosmos.

Creation In-depth:

EXTRA-SOLAR PLANETS

In the secular model of solar system formation, a cloud of hydrogen and helium gas begins to shrink and heat up. Much of the nebula collapses down to become the proto-sun which is surrounded by a disk

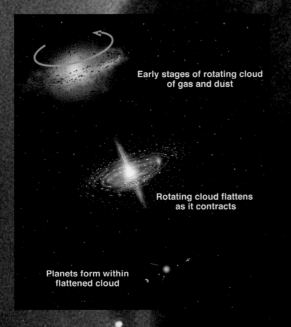

Early stages of rotating cloud of gas and dust

Rotating cloud flattens as it contracts

Planets form within flattened cloud

of gas and dust. The dust grains collect to form gravitational seeds of planets which grow larger as they absorb more gas and dust. Upon reaching critical density, the sun begins fusing hydrogen gas and the radiation drives away the hydrogen gas envelope surrounding the terrestrial planets. Since the radiation is weaker at greater distances from the sun, it is insufficient to drive away the hydrogen atmospheres of the outer planets. The model thus explains why the inner planets are small and rocky, and the outer planets are enormous giant gas worlds. Since other solar systems are thought to have formed in the same way, it was expected that they too would have small terrestrial planets orbiting close to the star, and large gas giants orbiting farther away.

We now know that this is not the case. Through various methods, astronomers have now discovered a number of planets orbiting other stars. In most instances, the planet has been detected by indirect means. Astronomers are able to measure the "wobble" that planets induce on the star they orbit; the orbit of the planet can then be deduced, even though the planet itself is not visible. The minimum mass of the planet can be estimated by the severity of the wobble. In a few known cases, the planet's orbit is aligned such that the planet passes directly in front of the star — blocking a small fraction of the star's light. These transiting cases allow us to know the size of the planet as well as its actual mass. More recently, extra-solar planets have actually been observed directly.

Virtually all of the extra-solar planets discovered so far go against the secular prediction. They are large gas giants which orbit very close to their star. They are often referred to as "hot Jupiters." To be fair, most of the techniques used to discover these planets could only detect hot Jupiters. Nonetheless, the fact that such systems exist in abundance is powerful evidence against the secular model.

As we might expect, secular astronomers have attempted to adjust their ideas of solar system formation to allow for the existence of hot Jupiters. One currently popular idea suggests that these solar systems formed so as to be much as our solar system is today — with gas giants far away from the star. Then the gas giants supposedly "migrated" from their original position to their current location close to their star. Unfortunately (for the naturalists), this scenario has many difficulties of its own. There are issues of how to stop the planet from crashing into the star once the migration begins. There is also the difficulty of explaining why this apparently did not happen in our own solar system. Rather than tacking on additional speculations to explain why the evidence does not fit the naturalistic expectations, might we consider the possibility that biblical creation is the correct explanation? These extra-solar planets are in line with the biblical world view. God has created a diverse universe with many types of solar systems for His pleasure, and to declare His glory as they are discovered (Ps. 19:1).

Although virtually all secular astronomers believe that stars form spontaneously, the physics behind this alleged process is riddled with difficulties. According to the standard model of star formation, stars form from a collapsing nebula. However, when gas is compressed, it heats up.[34] This higher temperature creates extra pressure which resists further compression. The collapse would have a tendency to stop before the star ever formed. Furthermore, a collapsing cloud would spin faster as it collapsed.[35] This is much the same way a skater spins up as she pulls her arms in. As the cloud spins faster, it becomes increasingly difficult to pull material in further: much as weights held at arm's length are difficult to pull closer when one is spinning. Even if the star were able to form by pulling in the material, it would be spinning extremely rapidly. A small percentage of stars do spin rapidly,[36] but most do not.

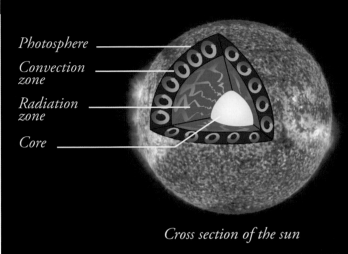

Photosphere

Convection zone

Radiation zone

Core

Cross section of the sun

The sun takes about 25 days to rotate once at its equator.[37]

There is also a problem with magnetic fields. The intrinsic (weak) magnetic field of the collapsing nebula would become intensified as the cloud collapsed; the process "concentrates" the magnetic field. The magnetic field would then resist being compressed further — much like trying to push two magnets together when their like poles are facing each other. Gas pressure, angular momentum, and magnetic fields all work against the possibility of a condensing star. Clearly, the secular view that stars can form naturalistically has some serious problems.

Earth

interpretations of the evidence, which then require further conjectures to allow the evidence to fit within the defective world view. When we start from a biblical world view, we find that none of the above issues are problems. On the contrary, they are assets. The seamless blend of uniformity and diversity that we observe in the created universe is a mark of the God of the Bible.

THE UNIQUE EARTH

From a creationist point of view, stars need not form at all. God made the stars (Gen. 1:14–16) during the creation week; they were supernaturally created.

Secular astronomers hope that future evidence will resolve these serious scientific problems, but not having enough evidence is not the real issue; it's the interpretation of existing evidence that is the problem. With these severe scientific problems (only a few of which have been discussed), should we not at least consider the possibility that the naturalistic world view is wrong? This incorrect world view has led to incorrect

We now move on to some other topics where the majority of astronomers are in opposition to a biblical world view. A very significant point of conflict between the secular view of the universe and the biblical view has to do with the uniqueness of the earth. In the secular view, the earth is (in a sense) "just another planet," albeit one where the conditions were lucky enough for life to form and evolve. The naturalist believes that the earth, along with the rest of the universe, is just a happy accident.

It is one planet among innumerable billions in our galaxy — with other galaxies having billions of planets of their own. Most secular astronomers believe that many other "earths" exist in the universe. If we assume that our planet is an accident of nature, and that billions times billions of other planets have also formed as accidents of nature, then surely some of these are bound to come out the same way earth did.

The Bible teaches the contrary: the earth is special. Earth is unique among all the worlds that the Lord created. The description of creation as recorded in Genesis 1 makes this abundantly clear. Five of the six days of creation are spent creating and forming the earth and the life on it. Only one day is spent creating the other objects in the universe. Undoubtedly, the earth is different.

In fact, the earth is three days older than any of the other planets and stars in the universe.[38] The earth was made on the first day of creation; God made it in the beginning (Gen. 1:1). The lights in the sky were made on the fourth day of creation. These lights are the sun, moon, and stars (both the "true" stars and the "wandering stars" — planets). Perhaps the Lord created the earth first to show its special significance in His divine plan.

Clearly, other planets do exist. There are several other planets in our own solar system besides earth, and astronomers have detected quite a number of planets orbiting other stars, and yet, our ability to detect extra-solar planets is still quite limited. It therefore seems very likely that there are countless billions of planets which have yet to be detected, but these planets are not merely accidents of nature. God created all these worlds for His pleasure (Rev. 4:11) and to declare His creative wisdom and glory to us. Since the other planets serve a different purpose than the earth, we expect that the planets will be different in nature than the earth. Science has certainly confirmed this biblical expectation.

Size comparison of the giant gas planets

Jupiter *Saturn* *Uranus* *Neptune*

(and Jupiter about 11 times) the earth's diameter. I have thoroughly enjoyed viewing these planets through telescopes. They are dynamic — particularly Jupiter and Saturn. The outer planets demonstrate God's inventiveness, but clearly they are very different from the earth. The extra-solar planets we have discovered so far appear to be much like these gas giants — large balls of hydrogen gas. They are beautifully made, but not like the earth.

The earth is unique among known worlds for a number of reasons. For example, the earth is the only planet known to have plate tectonics. The earth's crust appears to be divided into plates which can move relative to each other. This is very significant because the mechanism of plate tectonics is thought to be largely involved in the global flood described in Genesis 6–8. God used this flood to judge the sin of mankind (Gen. 6:11–13). Since the other planets did not need to be flooded, it stands to reason that they would not need plate tectonics.

Liquid water exists in abundance on earth; this is an extremely unusual condition. Although water molecules are fairly common in the universe, they are generally found in the form of vapor, or ice — not liquid. The fact that 70 percent of the earth's surface is covered with water is extremely exceptional. The earth has an abundance of free oxygen — no other known planet has an atmosphere like this.

Additionally, the earth is at just the right distance from the sun for life to be possible. Indeed, many of earth's characteristics are specially designed for life. This is exactly what we would expect from the Bible. God formed the earth to be inhabited (Isa. 45:18). That is the earth's primary purpose. The purpose of the rest of the stars and planets in the universe is different. The rest of the universe was made to divide the day from the night, to be for signs, seasons, days, and years (Gen. 1:14), to give light upon the earth (Gen. 1:15), and to declare God's glory (Ps. 19:1) for His pleasure (Rev. 4:11). The Bible teaches, and science confirms, that the earth is unique.

THE QUESTION OF EXTRATERRESTRIAL LIFE

The distinctiveness of the earth dovetails with a question that people often ask: "Are there extraterrestrial life forms out there?" The question of life from other planets is a hot topic in our culture today. Science fiction movies and television shows often depict strange creatures from faraway planets, but these ideas are not limited merely to science fiction programming. Many secular scientists believe that one day we will actually discover life on other planets. There are even programs like SETI (the Search for Extra-Terrestrial Intelligence) that scan the heavens with powerful radio telescopes "listening" for signals from intelligent aliens. Unfortunately, many Christians have bought into the idea of extraterrestrial "alien" life without critically assessing such a belief in light of Scripture.

The idea of extraterrestrial life stems largely from a belief in evolutionism. Recall that in the evolution view, the earth is "just another planet" — one where the conditions just happened to be right for life to form and evolve. If there are countless billions of other planets in our galaxy, then surely at least a handful of these worlds have also had the right conditions. Extraterrestrial life is almost inevitable in an evolutionary world view.

However, the notion of alien life does not square well with Scripture. As previously discussed, the earth is unique.

Imaginative artwork depicting alien life forms.

marine life to swim in the ocean on day 5, and animals to inhabit the land on day 6. Human beings are also made on day 6 and are given dominion over the animals, but where does the Bible discuss the creation of life on the "lights in the expanse of the heavens"? There is no such description, because the lights in the expanse were not designed to accommodate life. God gave care of the earth to man, but the heavens are the Lord's (Ps. 115:16). From a biblical perspective, extraterrestrial life does not seem reasonable.

Problems are multiplied when we consider the possibility of intelligent alien life. Science fiction programming abounds with "races" of people who evolved on other worlds. We see examples of "Vulcans" and "Klingons" — pseudo-humans similar to us in most respects, but different in others.

It is the earth that was designed for life (Isa. 45:18), not the heavens. The other planets have an entirely different purpose than does the earth, and thus they are designed differently. In Genesis 1, we read that God created plants on the earth on day 3, birds to fly in the atmosphere and

As a plot device, these races allow the exploration of the human condition from the perspective of an outsider. Although very entertaining, such alien races are theologically problematic. Intelligent alien beings cannot be redeemed! God's plan of redemption is for human beings: those descended from Adam. Let us examine the conflict between the salvation message, and the notion of alien life.

THE REDEMPTION OF MANKIND

The Bible teaches that the first man (Adam) rebelled against God (Gen. 3). As a result, sin and death entered the world (Rom. 5:12). We are all descended from Adam and Eve (Gen. 3:20) and have inherited from them a sin nature (Rom. 6:6, 20). This is a problem: sin is a barrier that prevents man from being right with God (Isa. 59:2), but God loves us (despite our sin) and provided a plan of redemption — a way to be reconciled with God.

After Adam and Eve sinned, God made coats of skins to cover Adam and Eve (Gen. 3:21). He therefore had to kill an animal(s). This literal action is symbolic of our salvation; an innocent Lamb (Christ — the Lamb of God) would be sacrificed to provide a covering for sin (John 1:29). In the Old Testament, people would sacrifice animals to the Lord as a reminder of their sin (Heb. 10:3) and as a symbol of the One to come (the Lord Jesus) who would actually pay the penalty for sin.

The animal sacrifices did not actually pay the penalty for sin (Heb. 10:4, 11). Animals are not related to us; their shed blood cannot count for ours, but the blood of Christ can. Christ is a blood relative of ours since He is descended from Adam as are we; all human beings are of "one blood" (Acts 17:26). Furthermore, since Christ is also God, His life is of infinite value and thus His death can pay for all the sins of all people. That is why only the Lord himself could be our savior (Isa. 45:21). Therefore, Christ died once for all (Heb. 10:10).

The redemption of ET?

When we consider how the salvation plan might apply to any hypothetical extraterrestrial (but otherwise human-like) beings, we are presented with a problem. If there were "Vulcans" or "Klingons" out there, how would they be saved? They are not blood relatives of Jesus, and so Christ's shed blood cannot pay for their sins. One might at first suppose that Christ also visited their world, and lived and died there as well, but this is anti-biblical. Christ died once for all (1 Pet. 3:18; Heb. 9:27, 10:10). Jesus is now and forever both God and man; but He is not an "alien."

One might suppose that alien beings have never sinned, in which case they would not need to be redeemed, but then another problem emerges: they suffer the effects of sin, despite having never sinned. Adam's sin has affected all of creation — not just mankind. Romans 8:20–22 makes it clear that the entirety of creation suffers under the bondage of corruption. These kinds of issues highlight the problem of attempting to incorporate an anti-biblical notion into the Christian world view.

Extraterrestrial life is an evolutionary concept; it does not comport with the biblical teachings of the uniqueness of the earth and the distinct spiritual position of human beings. Of all the worlds in the universe, it was the earth that God himself visited, taking on the additional nature of a human being, dying on a cross, and rising from the dead in order to redeem all who would trust in Him. The biblical world view sharply contrasts with the secular world view when it comes to alien life. So, which world view does the scientific evidence support? Do modern observations support the secular notion that the universe is teeming with life, or the biblical notion that earth is unique?

Where is everybody?

So far, no one has discovered life on other planets or detected any radio signals from intelligent aliens. This is certainly what a biblical creationist would expect. Secular astronomers continue to search for life on other worlds, but they have found only rocks and inanimate matter. Their radio searches are met with silence. The real world is the biblical world; a universe designed by God with the earth at the spiritual focal point — not an evolutionary universe teeming with life.

When it comes to extraterrestrial life, science is diametrically opposed to the evolution-

topic of extraterrestrial life when he asked the profound question: "Where is everybody?" Since there are multiple billions of planets in our galaxy, and since in the secular view these are all accidents, it is almost inevitable that some of these had the right conditions for life to evolve, and if some of these worlds are billions of years older than ours, then at least

Alien plants. Computer artwork depicting scientist's impression of alien plants shaped like balloons.

ary mentality. We currently have no evidence of alien life forms. This problem is not lost on the secular scientists. Allegedly, the atomic scientist Enrico Fermi was once discussing the

some of them would have evolved intelligent life eons ago. The universe should therefore have countless numbers of technologically superior civilizations, any one of which could

Artist illustration of Pluto, Charon, and the sun

have colonized our galaxy ages ago. Yet we find no evidence of these civilizations: "Where is everybody?" This problem has become known as the "Fermi paradox."

This paradox for evolution is a feature of creation. We have seen that the earth is designed for life. With its oceans of liquid water, a protective atmosphere containing abundant free oxygen, and a distance from the sun that is just right for life, earth was certainly designed by God to be inhabited. The other planets of the universe were not. From the sulfuric acid clouds of Venus to the frozen wasteland of Pluto, the other worlds of the solar system are beautiful and diverse, but they are not designed for life.

Sometimes after I speak on the topic of extraterrestrial life, someone will ask me about UFOs. A "UFO" (unidentified flying object) is just that — an object seen in the sky that is unidentified to the person seeing it. People often want me to explain a sighting of some unknown flying object which they (or often a friend) have claimed to see. (Sometimes the implication is that if I can't explain it, it somehow proves that it must be an alien spacecraft; but such reasoning is completely vacuous.[39]) These kinds of questions are unreasonable. It is one thing to be asked to interpret evidence that we have, but it is unrealistic to ask someone to interpret undocumented second or third-hand stories with no actual evidence available for inspection.

There is no doubt that some people sincerely have seen things in the sky that they do not understand. This is hardly surprising since there are lots of things "up there" which can be misunderstood to people not familiar with them. These include: Venus, satellites, the international space station, the space shuttle, rockets, Iridium flares, man-made aircraft, internal reflections, meteors, balloons, fireflies, aurorae, birds, ball lightning, lenticular clouds, parhelia, etc. However, a person unfamiliar with these would see a "UFO," since the object is "unidentified" to him or her. It is how people interpret what they see that can be questionable.

Remember that we always interpret evidence in light of our world view. It is therefore crucial to have a correct, biblical world view. The fallacious world view of atheism/naturalism may lead someone to draw erroneous conclusions about what they see. From a biblical world view, we expect to occasionally see things that are not easily explained, since our minds are finite, but UFOs are not alien spacecraft, and of course there is no tangible evidence to support such a notion.[40]

WHY THE HYPE?

In the 1990s, the television series *The X-Files* entertained millions of fans with stories of aliens, government conspiracies, and one dedicated FBI agent's relentless search

Radio telescopes listen for extraterrestrial life

for truth. The show's motto, "The truth is out there," is a well-known phrase for sci-fi fans. Why is there such hype surrounding the notion of extraterrestrial life? Why is science fiction programming so popular? Why does SETI spend millions of dollars searching for life in outer space?

The discovery of intelligent extraterrestrial life would certainly be seen as a vindication of evolutionism; it is an expectation from a naturalistic world view. The desire to meet aliens (especially intelligent, technologically advanced ones) seems much more deeply felt than merely to vindicate evolutionary predictions. What is the real issue? I've heard a number of different answers from secular astronomers.

In some cases, a belief in ETs may stem from a feeling of cosmic loneliness: "If there are aliens, then we would not be alone in the universe." In many cases it comes from an academic desire to learn the mysteries of the universe; a highly developed alien race might have advanced knowledge to pass on to us. Perhaps such knowledge is not merely academic; the

hypothetical aliens may know the answers to fundamental questions of existence: "Why am I here? What is the meaning of life?" And so on. An advanced alien race might have medical knowledge far exceeding our own: knowledge which could be used to cure our diseases. Perhaps their medical technology would be so far advanced that they even hold the secret of life and death; with such incredible medical knowledge, perhaps human beings would no longer have to die — ever.

In a way, a belief in extraterrestrial life has become a secular replacement for God. God is the one who can heal every disease. God is the one in whom all the treasures of wisdom and knowledge are deposited (Col. 2:3). God is the one who can answer the fundamental questions of our existence. God alone possesses the gift of eternal life (John 17:3). It is not surprising that the unbelieving scientist would feel a sense of cosmic loneliness, having rejected his Creator, but we are not alone in the universe; there is God. God created us for fellowship with Him, thus we have an in-built need for God and for purpose. Although human beings have rejected God (in Adam, and by our own sins as well), our need for fellowship with Him remains.

When I think of the majority of intelligent scientists who have studied God's magnificent creation, but have nonetheless rejected that God and have instead chosen to believe in aliens and millions of years of evolution, I am reminded of the words of Scripture. Romans 1:18–25 reveals that a rejection of God in favor of naturalism is not a new practice. God's invisible qualities (His eternal power and divine nature) are clearly revealed in the natural world so that there is no excuse for rejecting God (Rom. 1:20) or suppressing the truth about God (Rom. 1:18). The thinking of man apart from God is nothing more than futile speculations (Rom. 1:21). Exchanging the truth of God (such as creation) for a lie (such as evolution), and turning to a mere creature (such as hypothetical aliens) for answers is strikingly similar to what is recorded in Romans 1:25.

When we start from the Bible, the evidence makes sense. The universe is consistent with the biblical teaching that the earth is a special creation. The magnificent beauty and size of a universe which is apparently devoid of life — except for one little world where life abounds — is exactly what we would expect from a biblical world view. The truth is not "out there," the truth is in there — in the Bible! The Lord Jesus is the truth (John 14:6). So when we base our thinking on what God has said in His Word, we find that the universe makes sense.

Milky Way galaxy

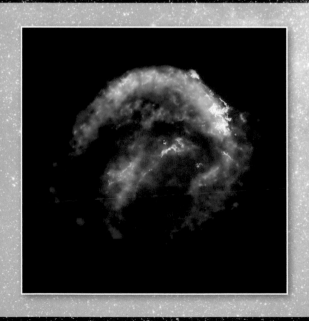

Kepler's supernova remnant is an expanding shell of hydrogen and helium gas 14 light-years in diameter. It is the result of a star that exploded in 1604 and was seen by many sky watchers — including creationist astronomer Johannes Kepler. This image is a false color composite from three spacecraft using different wavelengths of light: Chandra (X-ray shown as blue and green), HST (optical shown as yellow), and Spitzer (infrared shown as red).

The Helix Nebula (as it appears in ultraviolet light) is an expanding shell of hydrogen and helium gas. The central spot is a white dwarf — an extremely hot, dense object about the size of Earth. White dwarfs are often found at the center of such nebulae. They are thought to be the collapsed remnant of the star that produced the Nebula.

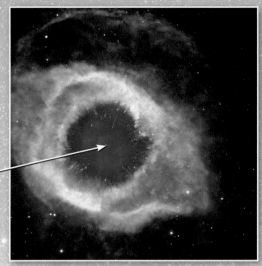

Helix Nebula

Cassiopeia A is a supernova remnant — the result of an exploding star. It is located about 10,000 light-years away in the constellation Cassiopeia. Although it is thought to be more recent than Kepler's supernova of 1604, this supernova appears to have gone almost unnoticed, perhaps because it was very faint. The sharp turquoise dot in the center is a neutron star. It is a hot, extremely compressed mass (no larger than a city) and is thought to be the collapsed core of the exploded star.

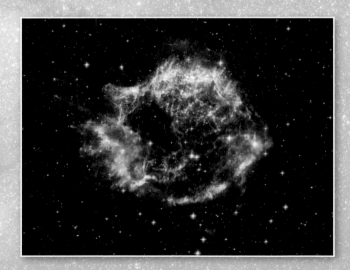

False color image of Cassiopeia A

CHAPTER FIVE

War of the world views

THE POWER OF A WORLD VIEW

A world view is inescapable. Our world view consists of our most basic assumptions (presuppositions) about reality. Our most foundational presuppositions (axioms) cannot be proved by something else (otherwise they would not be the most foundational), yet we hold them to be unquestionable. We use these assumptions (often without realizing it) to help us interpret what we observe in the world. We cannot avoid this; without a number of foundational presuppositions about reality we could not make sense of

anything. Consider a few assumptions that a typical person might hold to as part of his or her world view:

(1) I exist.

(2) There is a reality beyond myself.

(3) I have senses which can be used to probe that reality.

(4) There are laws of logic.

(5) I can use the laws of logic to draw accurate conclusions about the universe.

Most people would hold to the above assumptions (and many others as well, of course). We cannot actually prove them without making other assumptions, and yet we could not function without them. Suppose I see a small rock on the side of the road and I decide to pick it up. I have assumed quite a lot to take this action. I must have reasoned that (1) I exist — otherwise I couldn't pick up the rock. I assume that there is a rock — it is part of (2) a reality beyond myself. I have concluded that the image passed on to my brain by my eyes is an accurate representation of that reality (3). I have used logic to draw the conclusion (5) that I can pick up the rock; this means I have also presupposed that there are laws of logic (4). These assumptions are automatic; we don't even have to think about them. Yet, without them we could not know that it is possible to pick up that rock. These presuppositions (and others) constitute a person's world view. Clearly, a world view is essential in order to know anything about the universe.

How are we to know if we have an accurate world view? Is there any reason to think that our most basic assumptions about reality are correct? Although most people would agree on the five assumptions listed above, many people disagree on other very foundational ideas. These include: the existence of God, the nature of truth, the origin of the universe, the origin of life, morality, and many others. When people disagree on their most basic assumptions, how do we determine who has the more accurate world view?

Creation In-depth:

INTERNAL INCONSISTENCIES IN WORLD VIEWS

Some world views cannot be entirely correct because they are internally inconsistent. Consider the beliefs of a materialist. Such a person believes that all things are physical; nothing immaterial exists. The materialist uses reason and the laws of logic to support his beliefs, but he does so inconsistently. In his view, there can be no laws of logic since they do not exist physically. There is no place in the universe where you can "see" the laws of logic; they are intangible and thus cannot exist according to the materialists' professed beliefs. His reasoning is self-refuting.

Likewise, the evolutionist who believes that all life is merely an accidental by-product of chemicals, mutations, and natural selection has an internal inconsistency. Such a person must (by his own professed beliefs) accept that the human brain has developed accidentally. So why should we trust the brain's conclusions? We have no reason to accept assumption (5) in the list above if evolution is true. The evolutionist world view is therefore internally inconsistent. The evolutionist accepts assumption (5) to support his world view which does not comport with assumption (5).

The evolutionist might respond that natural selection has guided the brain so that it can determine truth. There is no reason to assume that that is true, because it does not logically follow that survival value equates with the ability to determine

truth. In fact, some incorrect beliefs might have survival value: for example, the belief that it is morally acceptable to do whatever I want (lie, steal, murder, etc.) as long as it increased my chances of survival.[41]

INCONSISTENCIES OF PRACTICE

Many world views lead to conclusions which are incompatible with the behavior of the persons who profess them. For example, a naturalist has no basis for an absolute moral standard, and yet most naturalists would nonetheless hold to a moral standard, and would be outraged if someone else were to violate it. If the universe is merely an accident, then what is the basis for right and wrong? What distinguishes a good action from an evil one in the naturalist's view?

For example, most naturalists would believe that murder is wrong. Why should that be so? By the naturalist's own assumptions, a human being is merely an accident of the universe. Why should one accident eliminating another be considered wrong? The naturalist can make up an arbitrary standard for morality (perhaps morality is determined by majority opinion, or inborn "feelings") but has no absolute basis for one. As such, he has no basis for imposing his mere opinions of right and wrong on others. Only a creation-based world view allows for the existence of absolute morality. If there is a Creator to whom we owe our existence, then that Creator can set the standards. The God of the Bible has created such standards — laws of morality which are absolute.[42]

ILLUMINATION FROM THE CREATED UNIVERSE

A person might argue that his or her world view is accurate because it can explain the scientific evidence, but all world views can do that — that's what they are for.[43] External evidence can never prove or disprove a person's world view in an absolute sense. The reason is simple: evidence is always interpreted in light of that person's world view. The evidence doesn't "speak for itself"; it's the interpretation that is significant, and the interpretation is bound to be compatible with the world view that produced it. This is inevitable.

As an example, consider the disintegration of comets discussed in chapter 3. Recall that comets cannot last for millions of years, and thus their existence supports the biblical age of the solar system. Does this refute the naturalist's world view (which holds to an age of the solar system of about 4.5 billion years)? The naturalist says, "Of course not. It simply means that there must be an as-yet-undiscovered Oort cloud (or genuine Kuiper Belt with numerous actual comet-sized objects) which produces new comets to replace the ones that decay." The naturalist has proposed an additional hypothesis which

Greek astronomer Claudius Ptolemy

and all the planets revolve around the earth. The geocentric model was strongly promoted by the Greek astronomer Ptolemy. Today, we hold to the heliocentric model — the idea that the planets (including Earth) orbit around the sun.[44] One might suppose that it would be easy to distinguish between these two models; simply watch how the planets move — examine the evidence.

The motions of the planets in the night sky are fully compatible with heliocentrism; the planets (and the earth) appear to orbit the sun. Such motions were well known in ancient times, but Ptolemy was able to explain these motions within the geocentric framework by the addition of supplementary assumptions. Ptolemy postulated that each planet orbits in a little circle which in turn orbits a larger circle centered on the earth.[45] The little circles are called "epicycles" and the larger circle is the "deferent." Thus, in Ptolemy's view, planets orbit the earth in a "spirograph" fashion — making little circles which move along a larger circle.

Amazingly, Ptolemy's geocentric model of

brings the evidence into line with his world view. Both creationists and evolutionists can do this with any evidence. Therefore, external evidence contrary to the expectations of a world view cannot strictly disprove that world view because one can always add on additional auxiliary (supporting) conjectures to bring the evidence into line.

Let's look at another example: Centuries ago, there was a commonly held belief called "geocentrism." This idea holds that the sun the solar system is able to predict the positions of the planets with a fair degree of accuracy — despite the fact that it is wrong.[46] By careful adjustment of the size of the epicycles and the speed at which the planets circumnavigate them, the observations can be explained within a geocentric framework. Of course, the heliocentric model can also accurately predict the positions of planets. Both models can explain the evidence and correctly predict future observations. The main difference is that the heliocentric model is far simpler; it does not require any epicycles at all,[47] and this is the lesson. The incorrect model required additional assumptions (epicycles) and adjustments to make it "fit" the facts. The correct model did not.[48]

Today, there are many similar battles between opposing frameworks of thought. There is creation versus evolution, billions of years versus thousands, naturalism versus supernaturalism, and secular humanism versus Christianity. As with the competing models of the solar system, these battles are not primarily about evidence; rather, they are about how such evidence is interpreted. When it comes to our world view, do we use the Word of God to interpret evidence, or do we use the opinions of fallible human beings?

A BIBLICAL VIEW OF THE

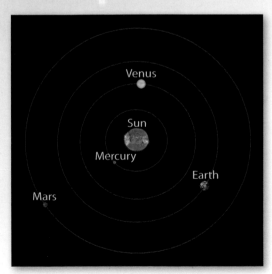

The heliocentric model of the solar system

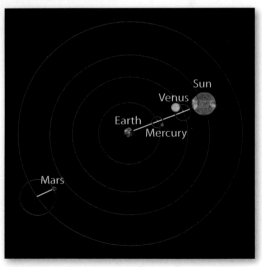

The geocentric model of the solar system

Orion Nebula

UNIVERSE

We have seen that when it comes to astronomy, the biblical world view makes sense of the scientific evidence in a straightforward way without the need for excessive arbitrary assumptions. In chapter 1, we explored how the vastness and beauty of the universe declare God's glory. God could have chosen to create only the earth, sun, and moon, and life would have been possible; but instead He chose to make a universe immense beyond imagination to give us just a small taste of His incredible magnificence.

In chapter 2, we saw that the Bible has always been right about astronomy. The sphericity of the earth which hangs on nothing, the expansion of the universe, the countless numbers of stars, the conservation principles of mass and energy, and the ordinances of the universe are all important astronomical concepts that are taught in the Bible. In many cases, the popular secular view of the day contradicted the biblical teachings, but the Bible has been vindicated.

In chapter 3, we saw how the biblical time scale is confirmed by scientific evidence. We understand that these evidences can always be interpreted in light of the secular view by the addition of extra assumptions (an undetected Oort cloud, spiral density waves, magnetic dynamos, etc.). We have also seen that there is no need for these conjectures in the biblical world view. The Bible provides a logical, self-consistent interpretation of scientific evidence supporting a universe that is thousands of years old. Conversely, the arguments offered in favor of the secular view generally assume uniformitarianism and/or naturalism and are thus circular.

In chapter 4, the secular belief in naturalism was challenged on both philosophical and scientific grounds. Problems with the secular big-bang and solar accretion models such as the missing antimatter, extrasolar planets (hot Jupiters), and star formation are in fact design features for creation — perfectly consistent with the Bible. The biblical implication that the earth is unique and that it alone harbors life is confirmed (so far) by observational astronomy.

We acknowledge that these evidences can be reinterpreted by the addition of untested assumptions. The atheist might assume that the universe really is teeming with life; we just haven't detected any yet, for whatever reason. The biblical world view makes sense of the evidence without the need for copious additional conjectures.

Nonetheless, a person who holds dogmatically to the secular world view will not be convinced by these evidences — nor by any evidences. There is a popular story about a psychologist treating a patient with a bizarre problem; the patient is convinced that he himself is in fact dead. The psychologist points out that all the medical evidence points to the fact that the patient is alive, and is in perfect physical health, but the patient remains unconvinced — pointing out that medical evidence can be misinterpreted.

Frustrated, the psychologist finally comes up with a plan to prove to his confused patient that he is in fact not dead. He asks the patient, "Do dead men bleed?" The patient replies, "No." At this point, the psychologist pulls out a small pin and pricks the patient's finger. A small drop of blood appears. "See! You're bleeding," says the psychologist, confident at having made his point (literally). The patient replies, "Wow!

The Bug Nebula, NGC 6302

assumption upon assumption in order to explain away evidence — evidence that is perfectly consistent with the biblical world view. How many supporting assumptions can a world view take? How many "epicycles" must we add before a person will consider the possibility that it may not be the evidence that is the problem, but the secular world view?

I guess I was wrong. Looks like dead men really do bleed, after all!"[49]

This story reinforces a profound truth. When a person is committed to a particular assumption or world view, no amount of evidence can change his mind, because the evidence can always be explained away by additional assumptions. Much of secular science has become like the "dead" man in the above tale. Secular scientists are well aware of the many problems with the big bang and secular models of solar system formation. Since they are unwilling to abandon the secular world view, they are forced to create

THE BIBLICAL WORLD VIEW

If we build our thinking on the Bible, the inspired Word of the God of the universe, then we have a correct foundation for an accurate world view. Only the biblical world view can provide a basis for logical thought and scientific inquiry which is self-consistent, makes sense of the scientific evidence, and provides an absolute moral standard. Notice that the five example assumptions at the start of this chapter are logically consistent with the Bible. I exist (1) because God made me (Ps. 139:14). There is a reality (2) because

God created it (Gen. 1:1). God created my senses (Ps. 94:9) so that I might be able to probe and master (Gen. 1:26–28) the reality He created (3). There are laws of logic (4) which we can use (5) (Isa. 1:18) because these were used by Jesus Christ. (As one example, Jesus used logic in Luke 24:39 when He argues that He cannot be merely a spirit because a spirit does not have flesh and bone which He does have.)

Although the unbeliever suppresses the truth of the Bible, he cannot help but borrow the above biblical principles. He inconsistently uses biblical truths while simultaneously denying the Bible from which these truths are deduced. For example, although there is no basis for believing that the mind can use laws of logic to reason in a naturalistic world view, the naturalist nonetheless knows that the mind can indeed reason. The Lord has "hardwired" us to be thinking creatures.

According to the Bible, God made human beings in His own image (Gen. 1:27). As such, we reflect in a finite, limited way some of God's infinite attributes. God is omniscient; He knows absolutely everything that is true. Thus, we can know some things. God is logical and self-consistent. Thus, we too can use logic and draw consistent conclusions. God has given us the ability to reason — to think some of His own thoughts after Him.

Although we have sinned, and now suffer the effects of the Curse, we still cannot help but know (on some level) that there is a God. His divine attributes are clearly seen in the universe He has made (Rom. 1:20). From the beauty of Saturn's rings to the majestic arms of the most distant spiral galaxies, God's character is displayed throughout the universe, and there is no excuse for dismissing this fact. The created universe tells us that that there is indeed a Creator God (Ps. 19:1–6) of infinite power and imagination. God's world confirms what we read in God's Word.

THE HISTORY BOOK OF THE UNIVERSE

Although the Bible is accurate when it touches upon astronomy (and everything else), its primary purpose is not to be a mere science textbook. The Bible is primarily a history book which shows us our place in God's universe and how to have a right relationship with Him. It is to be used as a guide — a "lamp" unto our feet (Ps. 119:105) giving us illumination to walk the path (Prov. 3:6) that God has laid out for us. God loves us and has created us for fellowship with Him. His desire is that we would love Him (Mark 12:30) and enjoy our life in Him (John 10:10).

God has not forced His fellowship on us; He gave mankind the freedom to choose to accept His love, or to reject it. In Adam, the human race chose to rebel against God, and the world was cursed as a result of Adam's sin. We, like Adam, have all sinned against God (Rom. 3:23) in various ways (Rom. 5:12–14), and the penalty for such rebellion against God is death (Rom. 6:23). We all deserve death and hell because we have sinned against an infinitely holy God, and since God is righteous, He must judge all sin — otherwise there would be no justice.

Since our shortcomings offend His infinite holiness, the punishment must also be infinite. Either we must suffer such punishment, or else a substitute must endure it in our place (Isa. 53). The substitute must be fully human to substitute for humanity (Heb. 2:14), and must be our blood relation (through Adam) so he can be our "kinsman redeemer" (Isa. 59:20, same word in Ruth 2:20). He must be perfectly sinless, too, so

He would not have to atone for sins of His own (Heb. 7:27), and must be fully divine so as to be able to endure God's infinite wrath (Isa. 53:10).

Fortunately, God did not leave us without a way back to a right relationship with Him. The second person of the Trinity took on human nature (Phil. 2:5–11), becoming the "last Adam" (1 Cor. 15:45), a descendant of the first Adam (Luke 3:38). Thus, He satisfies all the requirements for a substitute. Being both God and man, Jesus can also be our mediator (1 Tim. 2:5). Jesus Christ paid the penalty for sin for humanity (1 Pet. 3:18) by dying on the Cross. He took our place and died our death. The penalty for sin has been paid, and justice has been satisfied. We can be made right with God through simple faith and trust, via God's gracious gift, the sacrifice of His son (Rom. 6:23). We do this by confessing that Jesus is Lord and by placing our faith in Him (Rom. 10:9–10). Through this, our fellowship with God is restored. Even though we will all someday die physically (unless the Lord comes first), the Lord has promised that we will live again (John 11:25) forever in fellowship with Him if we believe on Him, grasping hold of His gift (Rom. 6:23). There is no way we could possibly earn this gift of salvation (Eph. 2:8–9); it is entirely by God's grace, received by faith.

Some people have the mistaken impression that God will let them into heaven without faith in Christ because they are "basically good." The Bible makes it clear that no one is "good" (Rom. 3:10; Ps. 14:3) because we all have sinned (Rom. 3:23).[50] If God were to let sin go unpunished, then there would be

that any should perish but that all should come to repentance" (2 Pet. 3:9). Nevertheless, some will reject His gift of grace, but if we reject God, then we are rejecting all that God is — peace, joy, eternal life. Therefore, we would be accepting suffering, hopelessness, a sort of eternal "death" — in other words hell. Hell is eternal existence apart from God's fellowship. Such an existence would necessarily be hollow, empty, and hopeless, because we were designed to be in fellowship with God. In this present life, our alternatives are either a relationship with God by receiving Jesus as Lord, or being separated from God, in effect rejecting Jesus. At death, God in a sense ratifies our choice (Heb. 9:27). The biblical world view is therefore much more than just a platform for scientific research. While it does provide

no justice. Furthermore, sin ruins paradise. Remember, it took only one sin (by Adam) to ruin the perfect world that God had created. God has said that He will in the future make a new heavens and a new earth; paradise will be restored. The new heavens and earth will remain perfect forever, which means not even one sin can enter in. Therefore, no one can enter heaven unless he or she has been the willing recipient of Christ's payment for sin. The Bible says that God is "not willing the foundation for good science, it also provides the basis for correct thinking about the Lord, origins, morality, and eternity. Only the Word of God can provide such a foundation. When we do science experiments, we do them in the present, physical universe; such methods are limited to the natural world. Based on his own experiences and empirical data, man can know nothing of the coming resurrection, or the nature of morality. It is only by revelation from the Lord (the Bible) that we can know these things with certainty.

CREATION ASTRONOMY

It has been said that astronomy is the least well-developed field in creation science. Far fewer creationist books and papers have been written in the field of astronomy than in the fields of biology or geology. This may be in part due to the fact that there are currently so few biblical creationist astronomers when compared to creation scientists in other fields. Yet, we have seen that astronomy strongly confirms what the Bible teaches,

and the secular alternatives are inadequate on multiple levels.

Still, there is a lot more to be discovered and there are unanswered questions in the field of creation astronomy.[51] When it comes to creation-based models of the universe, I am convinced that we have only scratched the surface. Future discoveries in astronomy will continue to confirm the Bible by exhibiting the power and ingenuity of the Lord in ways that we cannot yet imagine. I am also convinced that much of the astronomical evidence for biblical creation is *already known,* but has been misinterpreted because of a secular bias.

The quantity of astronomical data available today is staggering. The number of books and technical papers in the field of astrophysics is equally staggering, and yet, the vast majority of these are written from the fallacious world view of naturalism. This causes the interpretations of the data to be problematic, necessitating the addition of numerous arbitrary "secondary" assumptions. What is needed is to approach this existing information from a biblical framework.

This book is meant to be an introduction only — a starting point to a biblical view of the universe. We have shown how astronomy facts that are well known (recession of the moon, disintegration of comets, extra-solar planets, lack of antimatter, etc.) are strongly consistent with the Bible and problematic for secular scenarios. Many more such explorations are possible. Who knows what amazing truths are waiting to be discovered if only the shackles of secular thinking

*H*e counts the number of the stars;
He calls them all by name.

– *Psalm 147:4* *(New King James Version)*

are removed. Now is the time of discovery.

It is time to take back astronomy.

[1] On average, the moon's orbit is elliptical and so its distance from earth varies. Thus, its angular size varies somewhat. Sometimes the moon is slightly larger in the sky than the sun; at other times it appears a bit smaller.

[2] D. Faulkner, "The Angular Size of the Moon and Other Planetary Satellites: An Argument For Design," Creation Research Society Quarterly 35(1) (June 1998): p. 23–26.

[3] T. Snow, The Dynamic Universe, (St. Paul, MN: West Publishing Company, 1991), 4th edition, p. 528.

[4] Snow, The Dynamic Universe, p. 44.

W. Hartmann and C. Impey, Astronomy: The Cosmic Journey (Belmont, CA: Wadsworth Publishing Company, 1994), 5th edition, p. 44.

T. Snow and K. Brownsberger, Universe: Origins and Evolution (Belmont, CA: Wadsworth Publishing Company, 1997), p. 46.

[5] Of course, God can count the number of stars, and in fact does so according to Psalm 147:4. God has a name for every star, even though human beings cannot even count the number of stars.

[6] The order of magnitude of the estimate can vary slightly depending on the exact assumptions involved in the calculation.

[7] Hartmann and Impey, Astronomy: The Cosmic Journey, p. 52.

[8] D. Faulkner, Universe by Design (Green Forest, AR: Master Books, 2004), p. 15.

[9] I.e., it gives the age of the ancestor at the time the descendant was born, thus making the genealogy "watertight."

[10] http://www.answersingenesis.org/creation/v24/i2/herd_rule.asp

[11] George Wald (late professor of biology, Harvard University), "The Origin of Life," Scientific American (August,1954): p. 48.

[12] Many secular scientists are increasingly acknowledging the importance of catastrophic events in earth's history.

[13] The details, of course, differ. The big bang does not have a problem with distant starlight as such. Then again, biblical creation does not have a horizon problem. (The CMB does not need to start with different temperatures in a creationist cosmogony.) However, both problems are the same in essence: how to get light to travel a greater distance than seems possible in the time allowed.

[14] Eisegesis means reading things into the biblical text, as opposed to exegesis, understanding what the text is actually teaching.

[15] The day-age position has been thoroughly refuted in the book Refuting Compromise by Dr. Jonathan Sarfati (Green Forest, AR: Master Books, 2004).

[16]The fact that a dipole force produced by two objects on a third object is proportional to $1/r^3$ can be derived from a binomial expansion on the equation of gravity ($F=-GmM/r^2$). Such a derivation is available in many introductory physics textbooks on the topic.

[17]C.P. Sonett, E.P. Kvale, A. Zakharian, M.A. Chan, and T.M. Demko, "Late Proterozoic and Paleozoic Tides, Retreat of the Moon, and Rotation of the Earth," Science 273 (1996): p. 100–104.

[18]Ibid., p. 101.

[19]The creationist scientist James Clerk Maxwell discovered the four equations which govern the behavior of electric and magnetic fields. Magnetic fields are caused by electric current or a change in an electric field. Electric fields are caused by charged particles, or a change in a magnetic field.

[20]For this example, we neglect the effects that the Genesis flood would have had on the magnetic field. It is thought that the extensive and rapid tectonic activity associated with the Flood would have disrupted the circulating currents in the core, causing rapid, successive reversals of the magnetic field. Such an effect is consistent with alternating bands of remanent magnetism found by geomagnetic ocean floor surveys, for example. It is thought that such a process will cause a net reduction in the overall energy of the earth's magnetic field, thus causing it to decay at an accelerated rate. As such, it would only make the problem worse for a many-millions-of-years-old earth.

[21]D.R. Humphreys, "The Earth's Magnetic Field is Still Losing Energy," Creation Research Society Quarterly 39 (June 2002).

[22]D.R. Humphreys, "Reversals of the Earth's Magnetic Field During the Genesis Flood," Proc. First ICC, Pittsburgh, PA, 2:113-126, 1986.

[23]This has been suggested by Dr. Russ Humphreys in his article on "The Creation of Planetary Magnetic Fields" available online at: www.creationresearch.org/crsq/articles /21/21_3/21_3.html.

[24]There is evidence that the earth experienced temporary reversals during the Flood year due to the tremendous tectonic activity disrupting the circulation of electric currents in the core.

[25]D.R. Humphreys, "The Creation of Planetary Magnetic Fields," Creation Research Society Quarterly 21 (3) (December 1984).

[26]However, Pluto's magnetic field has not yet been measured. According to Dr. Humphreys' model, Pluto should not have an appreciable magnetic field.

[27]www.creationresearch.org/creation_matters/pdf/1999/cm0403.pdf, p. 8.

[28]In quantum physics, particles often behave as if they are rotating. This property is called "spin" because the particles possess angular momentum. This is similar to the

rotation of larger objects except that on the quantum level the angular momentum comes only in discrete quantities.

[29]Named after Dutch astronomer Jan Oort.

[30]This is because there is no "outside" or "beyond" the universe in the naturalist's view.

[31]In this context, "heavens" probably refers to the dimensions of the universe — the "fabric" of spacetime. The heavens would have been empty (at least of stars) for the first three days, since the stars were made on day 4.

[32]Biblically, planets are classified as "stars" — they are "wandering stars" and are referred to as such in Jude 1:13. The word "planet" means wanderer.

[33]See also *Dismantling the Big Bang: God's Universe Rediscovered,* by Alex Williams and John Hartnett (Green Forest, AR: Master Books, 2005).

[34]This follows from the ideal gas law. In physics notation, the law is written as $P = nkT$ where P is pressure, n is the number density of particles, k is the Boltzmann constant, and T is temperature in Kelvins.

[35]This follows logically from the conservation of angular momentum.

[36]T Tauri class stars, for example.

[37]The sun spins even more slowly at its poles (taking over 30 days to rotate once); thus, it is constantly "twisting" itself. This differential rotation would not be possible for a solid object, but since the sun is gaseous, it does not need to rotate at the same rate at all latitudes.

[38]This difference in age is as measured by clocks on earth. Einstein's theory of relativity has shown that time is not constant; time can flow at different rates in different regions of the universe. Time in the Bible must be from earth's perspective, since it is defined using day and night — a rotation of the earth.

[39]The argument is that alien spacecraft could not be explained by a natural phenomenon. Therefore, it is suggested that witnessing something that cannot be explained naturally must prove the existence of alien spacecraft. This is a logical fallacy called "affirming the consequent." It's equivalent to saying, "All white dwarf stars are white. Fred is white; therefore Fred is a white dwarf star."

[40]For a much more detailed discussion of aliens and UFOs from a biblical creation world view, see *Alien Intrusion: UFOs and the Evolution Connection*, by Gary Bates (Green Forest, AR: Master Books, 2004).

[41]http://www.answersingenesis.org/ Home/Area/feedback/2004/1217.asp.

[42]http://www.answersingenesis.org/ home/area/feedback/2004/1224.asp.

[43]However, not all world views can

provide a foundation for science and reason. Is there any reason to believe that the universe would obey orderly principles if it were simply an accident? Science depends on the fact that the universe is orderly and logical and conforms to uniform laws. Such properties are expected within a biblical world view, since a logical Creator constructed the universe and imposed order on it, but many other world views cannot account for these foundational axioms of science.

[44]To be precise, the planets and sun orbit about their common center of mass. However, since the sun is so massive, the center of mass between the sun and the earth is well inside the sun. Nonetheless, the sun "wobbles" slightly as the planets orbit it. Many extra-solar planets have been discovered by the "wobble" they induce on their star.

[45]In later geocentric models, the circle's center is offset slightly from earth.

[46]Of course, the issue of whether A orbits B or B orbits A is in a sense just a choice of reference frame (allowing "non-inertial" reference frames). However, when a third object is added, the symmetry is broken. Thus, the other planets definitely orbit the sun, not the earth. For example, Venus is sometimes in between the sun and the earth; at other times the sun is in between earth and Venus. This would not be possible in the Ptolemaic system.

[47]Today, we have many additional evidences that confirm the heliocentric model of the solar system: the phases of Venus, the moons of Jupiter, etc. are all difficult to explain in a geocentric view.

[48]The heliocentric model has, though, been refined by further adjustments that have improved its accuracy. For example, planetary orbits are better approximated by an ellipse than a circle. The physics of relativity has shown that a precessing ellipse is an even better approximation than an ellipse, and so on, but the basic framework has not changed.

[49]In fact, blood can be made to ooze for a while from a pierced fresh corpse. We could have said that the pin struck an artery, causing a fine pulsating spray of blood, but presumably most will take this as intended — a parable, not a physiology lesson.

[50]People who have never heard the Gospel are punished because they are sinners, not "because they haven't heard." They have the witness of creation (Rom. 1:18–28) and their own consciences (Rom. 2:14–16), so are "without excuse."

[51]There is not yet a consensus on distant starlight-however, big-bangers have a light travel-time problem of their own, and creationists have several possible models. We have yet to see a unified creation-based cosmology which will provide many of the scientific details on the origin and structure of the universe all within a biblical framework. We also need a detailed biblical model of stellar aging — how stars change with time.

Glossary

antimatter – a substance identical to ordinary matter except that the electrical charges of particles are opposite. I.e., an antiproton has a negative charge whereas a proton is positive.

astronomy – the branch of science that deals with celestial objects, space, and the physical universe as a whole.

astrophysics – the branch of astronomy concerned with the physical nature of stars and other celestial bodies, and the application of the laws and theories of physics to the interpretation of astronomical observations.

baryon – a class of particles that are composed of exactly three quarks. Baryons participate in strong nuclear force interactions and include such particles as protons and neutrons.

baryon number problem – the fact that the universe is matter-dominated, rather than having an equal amount of antimatter as would be expected if the big bang were true.

bias – prejudice in favor of or against one thing, person, or group compared with another, usually in a way considered to be unfair.

biblical creation – the origin of the universe, earth, and life according to a straightforward reading of the book of Genesis.

big bang – secular theory of the origin of the universe which proposes that all mass, energy, and space were contained in a point which rapidly expanded to become stars and galaxies over billions of years.

cosmic microwave background (CMB) – an invisible source of electromagnetic radiation (microwaves) which seems to be coming from all directions in space. Big bang supporters interpret the CMB as radiation left over from the big bang.

differential rotation – the condition in which different parts of an object rotate at different speeds; one example would be a spiral galaxy whose inner regions rotate faster than its outer regions.

dipole – a pair of equal and oppositely charged or magnetized poles separated by a distance.

doppler effect – an increase (or decrease) in the frequency of sound, light, or other waves as the source and observer move toward (or away from) each other.

electromagnetic radiation – a kind of radiation including visible light, radio waves, gamma rays, and X-rays, in which electric and magnetic fields vary simultaneously.

epicycles – a small circle whose center moves around the circumference of a larger one.

extra-solar planet – An extrasolar planet (or exoplanet) is a planet which orbits a star other than the Sun, and therefore belongs to a planetary system other than our solar system.

fusion – a nuclear reaction in which the nuclei of atoms combine to form more massive nuclei which releases energy in the process.

galaxy – a system of millions or billions of stars, together with gas and dust, held together by gravitational attraction.

general relativity – a theory of gravitation developed by Albert Einstein in which gravity is described as a geometrical curvature in space and time. One prediction of this theory is that gravitational fields slow the

Glossary

passage of time – a phenomenon that has been verified using atomic clocks.

geocentrism – having or representing the earth as the center, as in former astronomical systems.

heliocentrism – is the theory that the sun is at the center of the universe and/or the solar system.

inflation – a variation of the big bang theory in which the universe experiences an accelerated phase of expansion shortly after the big bang.

Local Group – the cluster of a few dozen galaxies of which our galaxy is a member.

magnetic field – a region around a magnetic material or a moving electric charge within which the force of magnetism acts.

materialism – the philosophy that all that exists is material.

Milky Way – a faint band of light crossing the sky, made up of vast numbers of faint stars. It corresponds to the plane of our Galaxy, in which most of its stars are located in the galaxy in which our sun is located.

naturalism – a philosophical viewpoint according to which everything arises from natural properties and causes, and supernatural or spiritual explanations are excluded or discounted.

plasma – an ionized gas consisting of positive ions and free electrons in proportions resulting in more or less no overall electric charge, typically at low pressures (as in the upper atmosphere and in fluorescent lamps) or at very high temperatures (as in stars and nuclear fusion reactors).

presupposition – a thing tacitly assumed beforehand at the beginning of a line of argument or course of action.

Ptolemy – Greek astronomer and geographer of the 2nd century A.D.

Pythagoras – c. 580–500 B.C., Greek philosopher; known as Pythagoras of Samos. Pythagoras sought to interpret the entire physical world in terms of numbers and founded their systematic and mystical study. He is best known for the theorem of the right-angled triangle.

redshift – the displacement of spectral lines toward longer wavelengths (the red end of the spectrum) in radiation from distant galaxies and celestial objects.

remanent magnetism – the magnetization left behind in a medium after an external magnetic field is removed.

singularity – the initial condition in the big bang theory in which the entire universe (including space, time and mass) is contained in an infinitesimal volume.

terminator – the dividing line between the light and dark part of a planetary body.

uniformitarianism – the theory that changes in the earth's crust during geological history have resulted from the action of continuous and uniform processes. Often contrasted with catastrophism.

Virgo Cluster – the massive cluster of about 2000 galaxies that lies in the constellation Virgo

world view – a particular philosophy of life or conception of the world: The Christian world view is based on the Bible.

Index

Index

Photo and Illustration Credits

Nasa: 5, 6, 7, 8, 9, 10, 11, 12, 13, 14, 16, 17, 18, 19, 21, 23, 24, 25, 26, 28, 32, 33, 34, 36, 38, 39, 46, 48, 49, 50, 51, 53, 54, 55, 56, 59T, 60, 61, 62, 63, 64, 70, 71, 72, 73, 74, 86, 88, 89, 90, 100, 101, 102, 108, 110, 111, 116, 117

Photos.com: 2, 7, 21, 36, 52, 97, 99, 112

Getty Images: 41, 45, 75, 76, 106

Bryan Miller: 29, 49, 61T, 85

Jason Lisle: 26, 27, 36, 44, 57, 59B, 66, 107

Corbis Stock Photography: 22, 77, 114

Science Photo Library: 19, 20, 30, 43, 67, 68, 69, 81, 83, 92, 95, 96

Science and Astronomy CD: 79

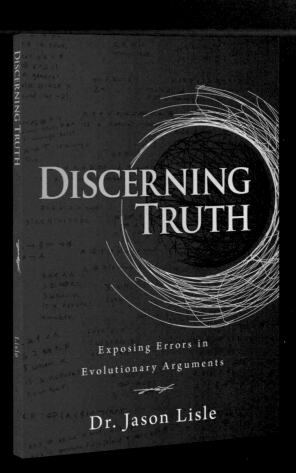